Initial Points in Politics

Using Our Constitution as
the Center of Politics

By Steven E. Maikoski
2009

For further information, contact:
Steven Maikoski
stevenmaikoski @ yahoo.com

ISBN: 978-0-615-34053-1

Cover Photo of U.S. Capitol at dusk by Steven Maikoski
Photo of author by Frances A. Miller

Contents

"Ambition must be made to counteract ambition."

— James Madison,
FEDERALIST NO. 51

Introduction

Our lack of a solid initial point in politics continues to bring a high cost to our nation and its good citizens.

With each session of Congress there are over 14,000 proposals put in motion by our senators and representatives; less than 300 of those thousands of bills will become law during their two-year session. A substantial number of those successful laws do little more than name federal buildings or post offices. Do the math; it's a terrible success rate. Perhaps it is one that we should be thankful for.

On average, some sixteen percent of the 14,000 proposals will seek to change a section of the tax code. Some of the proposed laws are so large that they are not read by the people who vote on them. Some bills are changed just before they receive a vote; portions may be added or subtracted and costly earmarks may be attached with little notice.

A few members of congress have tried to stop this legislative stealth; proposals have been introduced to bring "sunlight" on last minute changes to bills by placing a mandatory waiting time (often three or four days) between any change in a bill and the time that it receives a vote. The pause would give congressmen and citizens time to understand the contents of the changed bill.

But, Congress does not want this clarity; the sunlight proposal has died very time it has been introduced. What does that tell us?

Congress is wasting a lot of time, money and paper. But, we keep ending the same people back to D.C. so they can wage more of their varfare on accountability and performance.

his habitual mismanagement is a national problem that affects us all. . is a problem with Congress as a unit; it is a problem that crosses party nes. This book focuses on the problem, not the party. Therefore, this ook does not pander to the party faithful; there is no mention of any olitical parties herein.

Because of the lack of party identifiers, emotional content is not use to shepherd the party animal from one chapter to the next. The read will not receive the type of gratification that other books, politicia and news sources attempt to provide by saying that one's politic enemies are deserving of ridicule and punishment and one's favored po ticians are to be commended and rewarded. This book will instead be entertaining as a textbook on intermediate algebra or philosophy; it intended for the people who read such books and grasp that there a reasons for having such knowledge.

This book discusses how we think about politics. It questions wheth that process conforms to law or to other elements. It presents know edge that citizens should have concerning our political system and makes a study of the words and the positioning system we employ wh debating politics.

There is good reason for this discussion. Some time ago our system debating politics left its foundation and became inexact, assumptive ar circular. We need to return to the basics. Therefore, the readers w be asked to think beyond solutions that merely satisfy their financi stakes, emotions or personal philosophies. Foundations will be iden fied instead of assumed.

We will start by setting a couple of foundations, including a definiti for the first word itself: *politics*. To proceed in a logical manner we mu have a foundation, a consistent and solid definition of the word that w apply throughout this book.

Politics Defined:

People often say that what they view as the unwarranted promotion of an individual is due to politics. They may believe that favors were done, cash changed hands or family or love interests were involved — and they may be right.

But the word "*politics*" alone does not satisfy the full description of th action; there is more to the process.

Politics is the decision-making process itself; the reasons for thos decisions are independent of the term "*politics*." We can have persona politics, gang politics, party politics, company politics or family politics, to name a few.

For the purposes of this book, politics is defined as a process of deciding who gets what, how much they get, for how long they get it and when they get it. Among other things, the "*it*" may be money or fines, jobs or imprisonment, pleasure or torture.

Deciding who makes the decisions — the naming of an authority — is a political act as well. These decisions may be made from agreements, elections, assumptions or force.

One political decision will result in others. The direct election of any politician will empower them to appoint others into positions of political power. It is here where we see factional politics at its strongest and the results of honesty, or its absence, at its greatest.

How Politics Can Work:

When I was young our family lived in Levittown, New Jersey, where I had a paper route to cover my sixth grade expenses. While on that route one day I saw a fire starting to consume some brush that led to a small building. Running away from the scene was a boy of about ten years of age. I rode my bicycle over to the fire and beat out the flames with my jacket. As I stood looking over the area I could see a book of matches and a can of lighter fluid sitting nearby. In the distance the boy continued to run toward a housing tract.

decided to follow the boy home and tell his parents what he had done. ittle did I know that I was going to be given my first real lesson in olitical power plays.

Vhen I caught up to the firebug he told me to go away and leave him lone. I responded that I was going to tell his parents that he had started fire and then ran. As we approached his house he started yelling at me, hen crying and screaming for help. I was dumbfounded by his actions. had not touched the boy, but he was wailing as if I were hurting him. is tactics worked to his advantage; his father was out of the house and onfronting me in the blink of an eye.

When I told the father that his son had started a fire then ran from the growing blaze, the man did not care. Instead, he threatened me, saying that I was to stay away from his son if I wanted to live. His perception was that his boy was endangered by my presence, and he was going to save him from his "oppressor;" no matter what his boy had done, no matter who was right, no matter what laws were violated.

I rode off in anger, shocked but having learned from this lesson.

The firebug was a natural-born politician. He had committed a wrongful act, an actual crime, then turned the tables on the informer, making himself out to be the victim to the present authority, his father.

It is very important to note that when the father was informed of what his son had done he was unfazed. Never did he ask about the fire, where it was, what had happened, if anyone was hurt, what was burned, etc.. The man was so consumed with protecting his favored person that he did not care about the damage to any other person or property. Instead, he immediately engaged in family politics by attacking the person who sought to bring his son to a low level of accountability. To him, the only possible victim was his family, he had absolutely no cares or sympathy for anyone else.

Do these actions seem familiar? We have seen the same tactics and lack of concern in our political arena and in courtrooms across the U.S., and we will continue to see them.

In some cases, the actual truth may not matter to the guilty, the authority or some of the citizens; neither may criminal acts. Worse yet, those who honestly seek proper justice will most likely be personally attacked by the defendant, his loved ones or his cult following.

When the citizens allow it, truth will not matter as much as power. The proper authorities may do not act properly and many citizens may not care nor understand. These problems infect our entire system of government.

What does it take to change a corrupt system, especially when so many people, including the powerful, benefit from its processes?

Dissecting Opinions:

Opinion is another element covered in this book.

We can clarify the character of an opinion by breaking it down into three basic elements:

1. Direction – for or against; like or dislike
2. Intensity – the degree to which one holds that opinion
3. Certainty – the likelihood of change

The certainty is the interesting agent in his breakdown. A person may love sausage, but change his opinion after he sees how it is made. Additional knowledge is what usually changes an opinion.

The War on Assumptions:

Our modern sciences have shown how progress can be made. Possibilities and assumptions are used to develop a theory, which is then tested. From that point, we have knowledge and the system continues from there.

But most of today's political rhetoric is built upon assumptions as if they were facts; this is covered in the second chapter. From there, this book will develop foundations for political knowledge, party positioning, word use and rhetoric. In the final chapter, a possible solution for our political problems in tendered.

One Short Note:

Bold typeface is used to emphasize certain words. *Italics* denote references to specific terms, documents or acts. Quotation marks used on non-italicized words will indicate sarcasm.

1

Initial Points

"A point in every direction is the same as no point at all."

Harry Nilsson
quoting "the *Pointed Man*" in his
1971 album, "**The Point**"

Initial points are the most important references in our world. They are the starting point for any measurement of position, travel or time. Maps and directions mean nothing without an initial point; it is the "*You Are Here*" point on the map of the shopping mall, the rest stop on the highway or the map of the city. All ships and airliners plot their trips from their starting position, their initial point. The initial point is the start time for the note on the door that reads "Back in thirty minutes." The beginning of a ruler is its initial point.

An *initial point* is defined as a singular, finite, unique point that determines the base for other measurements.

Some *initial points* have become monuments. About four miles west of Portland, Oregon is a park dedicated to a marker known as the *Willamette Stone*, which marks the intersection of the Willamette meridian and the Willamette baseline. The Willamette Stone (now a stainless steel marker) is the initial point for all land surveys conducted and recorded in the states of Washington and Oregon. All properties and townships in those two states are measured from this one marker, this initial point. All other states have similar initial points as well.

Surveying is a serious business that uses a defined point of origin to determine property lines. Even if the surveyor's measurements were down to the millionth of a meter we would have terrible problems with property boundaries if there were no set initial point. The initial point is the main reference. It is not "living and breathing," it does not move with the times or with personal desires.

Okay, let's apply this seriousness to today's debates on politics. To become modern in our politics we need to understand and use the tools that have led the sciences to their many successes. Initial points are found in every successful science and in every stage of manufacturing that brings us our tremendous machines, yet few of us know of one in politics.

Politics Without An Initial Point:

I once listened to a national radio show in which the host and callers argued if some political views were either left or right of center; they did this without setting the initial point, i.e., the center for political measurements. How can anybody say something is left or right of center without defining a specific center, AND without explaining what characteristic makes an act left or right of center?

The well-respected talk show host continued the discussion with predictable results: Since there was no identified initial point, the show descended into the abyss of the subjective and useless arguments that pervades today's political discussions.

Without a defined initial point for our political system and our political debates, we will, predictably, have endless arguments and endless problems.

Setting a Proper Stake in Politics:

A basic political graph would survey elements from the center — the initial point — to the various distances on the left or the right. This system is what most of us use when claiming that something is *extreme right wing* or *leftist*. But how can we define the center? What determines the initial point that would establish the foundation for the *left* and the *right*?

The initial point can be determined by several elements, such as personal viewpoints, factional ideologies, party politics, or the laws of the United States.

When the initial point is established by party politics or personal preferences, it can change at any time with the desires of the parties; it can disregard ethics or current law. Its character would be inconsistent, delivering a graph open to any definition concerning what is left or right, or how far from center a political viewpoint sits.

If the initial point, the center, is determined by law we would have a better foundation. To establish this initial point we would simply use the origin for all laws in our nation: the Constitution of the United States.

Once we have a *Constitutional Initial Point* (Center) established, we can plot the party or person's views from there.

The details of a Constitutional center will be covered in another chapter, but first we must study the importance of such a defined center. To properly portray its importance, it is best to illuminate the weaknesses brought about by the absence of a solid initial point and to present the knowledge that is necessary in order to understand a *Constitutional Initial Point.*

2

2,300 Years of "Modern" Politics

"...men change their rulers willingly, hoping to better themselves, and this hope induces them to take up arms against him who rules: wherein they are deceived, because they afterwards find by experience they have gone from bad to worse."

Niccolo Machiavelli
The Prince (1513)

While reading Plato's "The Republic" I realized that the political problems of his day were much the same as those we enjoy now. Yet, we call ourselves "modern."

We really can't blame ourselves for thinking we are modern. After all, we are modernized by the conveniences of indoor plumbing and air conditioning, by the modern technologies of supercomputers, jumbo airliners and manned spacecraft, and by the advancements in modern medicine that enable open heart and cosmetic surgery. Our modernization has also delivered machines that provide on-demand entertainment, worldwide communication and information on global positioning. The fields of science and engineering have produced machines that have advanced our lives, but, politically, we suffer from the same old problems that have been haunting us for thousands of years. As Gary Seven, a character in the old-futuristic *Star Trek* series noted, our political progress has not kept pace with our scientific progress.

Gary Seven's *Star Trek* episode aired in the late 1960's, yet his observation that politics had not kept pace with science was nothing new even then. Such a story is part of a seemingly never-ending saga that has been repeated in books, plays and movies throughout the millennia. Our technology grows while our politicians continue to argue. Our technologies are modern; our politics are not.

People like to think that they are **modern** or **intelligent** beings, so these two words are frequently used as tools of persuasion to romance the buyer into purchasing an item; or, in political cases, a voter into supporting a candidate, a political cause or form of government.

When modern is applied to technology, medicine or science, the modern gizmo's performance may be measured against that of any previous version, so we trust that *modern* indicates an improvement over the earlier mode. When the term *modern* is used in politics we may not know if the change (if there is a change) is for the better, the worse, the new or the old.

What is *modern?* Several of the most respected political writers in history have referred to their own times as modern. Aristotle penned his views on modern politics some 300 years before the birth of Christ. Another political writer, Niccolo Machiavelli, mused about modernized thinking 500 years ago in "THE PRINCE." And, in the late 1780's, our founding fathers believed their writings represented modern political thought.

Human Faults:

Writings through the centuries reveal two very interesting points: first, that politics is infinitely corruptible because its great power is combined not only with the good intent of man, but with his ambition, greed and dishonesty as well, and second: that the people of today argue politics with the same assumptions, pride and party spirit that have been in play since the times of Aristotle and Plato.

As a result of these continuing practices, some of the most educated and enlightened versions of our current "modern man" render tremendously different opinions on what constitutes good government.

Not only do these people's opinions differ, but the intensity of their emotions can also be at the highest levels. Accusations of stupidity, partisanship, dishonesty and incompetence, as well as the most horrible political comparisons possible (e.g. Hitler, Gulags), now infect political arguments, even ones between family members or good friends. The sharp words, insults and vitriol present in some arguments can result in situations becoming as bad as they can be without turning violent.

These differences persist despite the fact that we now have a near-perfect system of distributing knowledge. With our innumerable education and information sources, today's modern man should be the most knowledgeable and advanced political creature in history, but he is making the same political mistakes that have been made for over 2,300 years.

When Aristotle wrote of politics, he did use the term modern to describe politicians, designs and writers. However, in his writing about ethics (Nicomachean Ethics) he never used the word modern.

All this brings up an important question: How can the same gray matter and neurological wiring allow today's politics to languish while our science greatly advances?

The answer is quite simple: Each field is treated differently.

Different Measurements:

Technological communications are defined in a precise, objective manner. They work from a disciplined process to strict identifications.

Political communications are flowing and subjective; they have variable rules and multiple definitions that change with the person.

True science uses a process that builds from one fact to another, giving it a dignity that separates it from other processes. The scientific process is hard to maintain and easy to violate.

Politics involves processes that may or may not have firm foundations. If popular opinion is the guiding force of a government, the determination of right and wrong is left to the opinion of the empowered majority. If emotion is the guiding force, such as when citizens follow their beloved leader, that leader determines what is right or wrong.

True science has specific definitions and established procedures to ensure its continued validity.

Politics still argues over its basic definitions and its endless legal processes as it has for two and a half millennia.

Identifying our Process — It Is Not Scientific:

Before we suggest any changes in the way we argue politics, we must first set a baseline by properly identifying the current process.

Our system of political debate is one that reflects the great degree of liberty we enjoy in this nation. It is a process that allows a person's own feelings and perceptions to guide his or her judgments. It is a process that can punish one person for a crime while allowing another to be excused for the same offense. It is a process that allows some people to blame one party for the ills of the nation while ignoring or pardoning the sins of their favored party. It is a system that allows the beauty or the ugliness of the party or the politician to rest in the eyes of the beholder.

That last sentence holds the key.

If a system caters to personal whim and free expression, and cannot withstand the disciplined procedures that lead to scientific validity, it will fall into another philosophical niche: the *artistic* system.

The *artistic* system gives people the license to disagree on any subject, as they will in regards to their opinions on the best painting, the best car or their favorite food.

An *artistic* political system allows for opinions based on some law, some truth, some science, some speculation, some falsehood, some hope, some love and even some hatred. So, it allows for personalized definitions, for personalized systems of law, for personalized enforcement of the law and for personalized judgments.

In politics the non-scientific methods of the *artistic* system enable people to call others *radicals, bigots* or *extremists* with no measure of the true sense of the words or any comparison with their own shortcomings. With an *artistic* system, the judgment is in the eye of the beholder. Individuals are empowered to judge others however they wish, even if their own points are refuted or unjust.

To the patrons of artistic politics, opinions are simply personalized views that are subject to a person's artistic sense; therefore, it is in their nature to dismiss the arguments of others as being the same; i.e. subjective and personalized. Law may not matter. It is one personal opinion versus another.

When constitutional validity is absent, the artists must rely on emotion, ego and popularity as tools of persuasion and validation. This spirit is heard in mass demonstrations, in cries for more rights and in portrayals of victimhood. Since the number of people often counts for greater validation than the proper role of science, government or laws, opinion polls become important tools in *artistic* politics.

Moreover, the use of an *artistic* system allows every foundation of government to be in flux when it is claimed that words, laws or rules are "living and breathing." This artistic tactic has the power to invalidate every law in government and every custom in society.

In short, an *artistic* political system enables individuals to draw every political picture any way they want, just as an artist could.

Short of Science — Longing for Logic:

The human element makes it impossible for politics to be brought to a fully scientific level, but being fully *artistic* leaves unlimited opportunities for serious problems to occur and fester. Therefore, it is reasonable and vital that some solid definitions be applied to our political communications. As a later chapter shows, it is easier than you may think.

We already have some solid political definitions established within our society. Our very own *Constitution* addresses the need for such definitions and principles in *Article I, Section 8,* where it gives Congress the power to "*fix the Standard of Weights and Measures.*" The nation has accepted firm and unchanging definitions for the quart, the inch, the ounce and the pound — and for very good reason.

Consider the manipulation and confusion that would result if each gas station in the United States took its lead from our political system and had its own "living and breathing" definition for a *gallon*. Some stations could sell their product for a dollar a "gallon" if they used their artistic sense to rename a quart, or a fraction of a quart, a "gallon."

As greed would spread, consumers could respond with their own artistic renderings of measurements by claiming that **their** "gallon" consists of six quarts, and demand that quantity from the producer for **his** advertised per-"gallon" price.

Although this tactic and wordplay would hurt some undeserving individuals, the *artists* could end up profiting from their system — and that is all that matters to some people.

Despite the large financial and life-and-death issues that politics covers, its heavily artistic nature and lack of a firm foundation is acceptable to people who profit from the current system or who will profit from further manipulation.

Roadblocks and Resistance:

Improvement requires change. But attempting change in any system is an invitation to resistance, especially when personalities, teams, money or power are involved — and politics has them all.

The resistance to any change in our system will be intensified by another problem: trust. Our government has grown so large and complex that many people have stopped trying to educate themselves about its processes. As a substitute for knowledge, they use a system of short-cuts, whereby they place trust in politicians, educators, news sources, special interest groups or political parties for political guidance in much the same way that some people seek out priests, pastors, cults or religions for spiritual guidance.

There is a danger in the resulting group-think. If the short-cuts become personal bonds instead of measured trust, a person will often follow the political leader, the spiritual leader or the political/religious cult group-think instead of following the altruistic intent of a government or church. The perils of such blind devotion are echoed from Munich to Jonestown.

In other words, being objective and embracing clarity in politics is a very good thing for any society.

Breaking through the Organized Resistance:

Having a good plan is not enough. You have to find a way to get people to listen to and understand it. The country's founders realized this with their new Constitution.

Once the activist is successful enough to get past the indifferent masses they will encounter some very determined obstacles to the spiriting of any true improvement in our political system. One obstacle will be the substantial group who fears changes in our system while claiming "we have always done it this way." Such resistance to change is as silly as advocating change for the sake of change alone.

Another obstacle is faced when the activist argues with persons who have considerable pride and identification invested in their political viewpoints. This group will include those who claim to have intellectual superiority over others and the followers who place a near-religious trust in their political party or their leaders. These people will defend their leaders and political opinions with the same vigor as some people would when defending a threatened family member or a sacred religious text. It is at this level where arguments may first depart from reasoned debate in order to engage in personal attacks.

But the most powerful obstacle to change in our political system is formed by the current political power-players, because any reformation in politics will affect their powerbase.

History has proven that when scientific advancements or reason conflict with the beliefs of groups of people, such as governments, political organizations, religions, churches, cults, factions or a combination of thereof, the people who profit from that current system — the power players — will fight in every way possible to keep their high positions and benefits within the status quo.

When these powerful people are unable to defend their positions with truth, they **will** do it with many other tools, such as half-truths, claims of intellectual superiority, projection, accusations against the "heretics" and story-telling that is designed to reinforce the faith and team spirit of their followers.

Effective use of these tools will lead their followers to believe that they are, or will be, victims of a competing group. This tactic is very powerful; it can cause some terrible injustices by punishing people (either through legalities or uncivil acts) who have not committed crimes.

> "Among the most formidable of the obstacles which the new Constitution will have to encounter may readily be distinguished the obvious interest of a certain class of men in every State to resist all changes which may hazard a diminution of the power, emolument, and consequence of the offices they hold under the State establishments; and the perverted ambition of another class of men, who will either hope to aggrandize themselves by the confusions of their country, or will flatter themselves with fairer prospects of elevation from the subdivision of the empire into several partial confederacies than from its union under one government."
>
> **Alexander Hamilton**
> Federalist 1

Because of such political power plays, even science has had trouble being scientific. When Galileo Galilei brought forward evidence that was in conflict with the teachings of the Catholic Church, he was put on trial by the Church's leaders in much the same way that others today are put on trial by politicians and their media cohorts for political purposes. Galileo had the bravery to question those in power, which, in turn, threatened the foundation of their power and the source of their income. So the power-players needed to discredit his findings and his character in order to keep their riches.

Because of his scientific mind, Galileo was placed under a sort of a house arrest, but his findings were correct and science eventually marched forward.

Today's politics uses similar tactics. It is in the financial interest of a party or church to squelch any progress in politics or science that conflicts with any facet of their organization's power and wealth.

Repulsive Reality:

A great American "philosopher," W.C. Fields, once said that there will come a time in every man's life when he must grab the bull by the tail and face the situation. If we grabbed the tail of our political animal we would see that today's situation involves the increased size, power, and perverted use of our government. There is nothing modern about it. Our current government is simply a repeat of all the other governments in history that have grown away from their original design and accountability. The power-players and their enablers are responsible for this situation.

Applying Logical Processes to Politics:

If we are to become truly modern in our politics, we must work to embrace the same logic and clarity that our successful sciences have used to develop our modern machines and medicine.

We do not need to go into deep formulas, but we do need to identify and use consistent elements. The field of chemistry provides an excellent example of clarity; it has precisely identified 117 elements. We find no such agreement on any single word in politics.

Russian chemist Dmitri Ivanovich Mendeleev is credited with establishing the beginnings of the periodic table of the elements in 1869. Throughout the entire world, the science community uses this Table as a foundation for identification and communication. As a result, consistent definitions cross national borders and languages; the elements identified as copper, zinc and helium mean the same thing to a chemist in Norway as they do to a chemist in Brazil. This definitive process was developed over one hundred years ago. The table follows logic, not politics, not art.

The table of the elements stands in contrast to the rhetoric in current "modern man's" politics. We argue over elements such as *conservative, liberal, progressive, socialist, republic* and *democracy.* We argue over the positioning of what is *left, right, center,* or *extreme.* Without any resolution in these matters, the foundation for political conversation is as stable as quicksand.

The result of a constantly shifting foundation is as predictable in building structures as it is in building governments: instability that can lead to damage or collapse.

The political parties involved in our modern political arguments are not using the same definitions, the same understanding of law or the same foundation of government when they formulate their opinions. Our debate is like a band in which each section plays at its own tempo and follows whatever music it desires, then claims that the others are at fault.

In our political arena, one side believes in keeping government within its constitutional bounds; the other side believes in changes — from small deviations to the absolute overthrow of our constitutional design. This is why we have these incredible differences in our political viewpoints.

Deviations for Profit:

The adherents to an artistic system, who have managed the deviations from constitutional intent, have been quite successful, for the bulk of today's federal government is made up of programs and powers that are unsupported by our founding document. Some of these deviant programs are very large; Social Security, welfare, unemployment compensation, medical care and education involve programs that are outside of our original constitutional design.

Some of our first politicians experienced the lure of such profitable deviations. Our nation's new government was hardly two years old before some legislators tried to expand its federal powers and influence beyond the original design. It was then that founding father James Madison rose to speak against a proposal that would have involved the government in the general welfare of businesses. As you read his remarks you may see that our government has since grown into the monster that Mr. Madison precisely described:

> *"If Congress can employ money indefinitely to the general welfare, and are the sole and supreme judges of the general welfare, they may take the care of religion into their Own hands; they may a point teachers in every state, county, and parish, and pay them out of their public treasury; they may take into their own hands the education of children, establishing in like manner schools throughout the Union; they may assume the provision for the poor; they may undertake the regulation of all roads other than post—roads; in short, every thing, from the highest object of state legislation down to the most minute object of police, would be thrown under the power of Congress; for every object I have mentioned would admit of the application of money, and might be called, if Congress pleased, provisions for the general welfare."*
>
> — ***James Madison*** *in the House of Representatives, February 3, 1792, speaking on the Cod Fishery Bill and granting bounties*

Our eventual fourth president saw the danger of big government growth and he protested. Now, two hundred years later, almost everything he fought against is entrenched in our system.

The deviations present in today's government are the source of an incredible amount of power and money for some citizens and politicians. Expect these millions of beneficiaries to protect their treasure with all the spirit they can muster.

Reset:

If we reboot our political egos and make a principled effort to study the workings of our current operating system — the Constitution — the task to understand today's politics will become easier. Just as students cannot learn algebra until they learn simple math, citizens cannot understand our politics unless they first understand the foundation of our government. Therefore, the next chapter focuses on some vital facts that every voter should know. The discussion thereafter will move to elements and structure.

3

Necessary Knowledge

> "No people will tamely surrender their Liberties, nor can any be easily subdued, when knowledge is diffusd and Virtue is preservd. On the Contrary, when People are universally ignorant, and debauchd in their Manners, they will sink under their own weight without the Aid of foreign Invaders."
>
> **Samuel Adams**
> 1775

In their quest to establish a better nation, our founding fathers studied many governments, from the ancient Achaean and Lycian Leagues to their own Federation of American States. They welcomed systems that worked, avoided those that didn't and established some safeguards against the continuing challenges brought by human nature.

The founders had been warned by history that any venture that involved humans would have problems, and that the best governments would fail if the people of the nation — both the citizens and politicians — lost their virtue or their understanding of the respected duties of the government and its citizenry. The founders worked to bring about the best government ever designed by man. We should do our best to understand it.

Their new Constitution gave our nation a government that allowed liberty to flourish, but did not give citizens or the government absolute liberty. Liberty must have its limits; we have free speech up to a point, free press up to a point, privacy up to a point, and so on. Their design gave government its own limitations of power, most of which are specified by the *Bill of Rights.*

Know How:

It is important to understand a system if we are to participate in its workings. Operators should know how their machines work; citizens should know how their government works.

A person who does not understand a system will tend to rely upon the opinions and guidance of others — i.e., self-interests, party politics and charismatic follow-the-leader systems — or, worse still, they will vote for the person or system that caters to their pride or satisfies their greed or need for revenge.

Such systems are becoming commonplace in today's arena. Some writers have referred to contemporary TV-ready, teleprompter-reading politicians as "charismologists." From their clothing that is chosen to suit the occasion to their cosmetic surgery and choreographed head and hand movements during a speech, these politicians are the new product of and for the modern media.

Our founders were far different than today's characters. James Madison, our fourth president and the man known as the *Father of our Constitution*, stood barely five feet tall and had a soft, unimpressive voice. His absence of "gravitas" would never have allowed him into any of today's political offices, where appearance, platitudes and choreography mean more than knowledge, content or virtue.

However, Madison, as well as the rest of the country's founders, used their know-how to develop a particular construction of government. There was an interrelationship between the different branches that established a balance in its design. What would seem to be a small change in one part could have strong consequences in other parts.

Basic Types of Governance:

The few items that will be covered in this chapter are important. They should be understood before a person puts on the political referee's uniform and starts calling fouls. We need to start with some basic items.

- **No government** — There is no formal law. This could be a state of anarchy, in which the greater might wins, or, it could be a uniform honest and crime-free society, known as a utopia. This necessitates a short note:

  A homogenous political culture that is benevolent in nature will not have conflict and will not need elections or laws. However, that utopian ideal is crushed by the inherent nature of our species: Man has a great ability to be greedy and dishonest. We will find dishonest and crafty characters within our families, workplaces, education systems, political organizations, governments and religions. Any organization or activity that depends on trust or empowers people will attract the honest and the dishonest alike. Some people will seek office out of a sense of duty while others will wish to reap personal gain from the environment of trust and the distribution of power.

  Lost in the environment of trust is the fact that any dishonest character, group or religion will not advertise itself as dishonest or evil; instead, it will adopt an altruistic pose and promise rewards in exchange for trust. From the earliest times in history, political systems, churches, benevolent organizations and families have contained people who have, to varying degrees, a mixture of dishonest, crafty and altruistic characteristics. The good citizen's hope for utopia can end up playing into the hands of the dishonest.

- **Government of liberty and law** — A form of government that allows society to run on its own for the most part, but holds a set of laws and enforcement processes to ensure fairness in its citizens' dealings. Its most important duty is to defend the nation from invasion and rebellion. Apart from that, the government's involvement in citizens' lives and state issues is minimal. Because of this, a great deal of respect for the law, the rights of fellow man and fair play is required of the citizens. Therefore, it is necessary for those in government to be held to the highest levels of honesty, good character and accountability by the politicians themselves, the voters and the reporting media.

The various local governments are left with a great deal of latitude in dealing with many issues, allowing citizens to seek friendly harbors for their own ways of life without having to deal with constant, and possibly heavy-handed, government involvement.

- **Providing government** — Government is the provider of services and/or goods, and, in extreme cases, life itself. This highly active form of government constantly grows in size, complication and power. As it grows, the liberties of its citizens shrink relative to the increasing needs or desires of the government.

  The natural law for a providing government is this:

  > **For the government to give to some,**
  > **it must first *take* from others.**

  The providing government can **take** through taxes, partial or complete confiscation, the nationalization of industries or resources, enslavement of citizens or nations, various acts of war, or any combination of these acts. If the government does not **take** enough from others, its expenditures and liabilities will force it into debt and, ultimately, bankruptcy.

  Citizens and businesses eventually become greater servants to the master government as its needs increase because of bureaucratic bloat and an ever-growing number of idle or semi-idle beneficiaries. The benefits of private-sector accomplishment are minimized in this form of government, and the politicians' ability to deliver services or favors in return for their election is **maximized**. Worse still, politicians are put in a position where they can encourage problems in the nation then offer a government "cure" for the difficulties that they have caused or exacerbated.

Once this system of political payoff begins within a government of liberty, the greed of the many voters will take over and the movement will metastasize, spreading selective punishment and benefits until it causes the original government to wilt, and in a matter of time, die.

"The Seductive Lure of Socialism: Here I encounter the most popular fallacy of our times. It is not considered sufficient that the law should be just; it must be philanthropic. Nor is it sufficient that the law should guarantee to every citizen the free and inoffensive use of his faculties for physical, intellectual, and moral self-improvement. Instead, it is demanded that the law should directly extend welfare, education, and morality throughout the nation.

This is the seductive lure of socialism. And I repeat again: These two uses of the law are in direct contradiction to each other. We must choose between them. A citizen cannot at the same time be free and not free."

Frédéric Bastiat
The Law, 1850

There are other types of governments whose processes place them somewhere within these highly different models. But these are the fringes of possible governments; we will work with them for now.

Back to School:

As I gathered information to write this book I must say that my greatest surprise was when I realized that today's public education systems deliberately under-educate the citizens about their government. Why are they doing that?

I once went to my old college and informally asked passing students a few questions. After a little over two hours and 51 responses, I had some data that agreed with my questioning of other people over several years: Nearly all the registered voters that I had talked to did not understand the basics of our government. The <u>one</u> college student who gave me correct answers for two of these questions learned the information from his family, not his school.

Here are the questions I asked:

1. What form of government do we have in the United States?
2. What is the only guarantee in the Constitution?

3. What was the purpose of the Federalist Papers and who were the writers?

These elements are part of the foundation of the government of our United States. Strangely, average citizens do not know the correct answer for any one of these questions.

Answers:

The *Pledge of Allegiance* is given to the *republic, for which it stands.* Our form of government is a **republic**. In no place does our Constitution mention the word democracy. As a matter of fact, our founding fathers purposefully avoided a democratic form of government because history had proven it to be a terrible system.

> "A common passion or interest will, in almost every case, be felt by a majority of the whole; a communication and concert result from the form of government itself; and there is nothing to check the inducements to sacrifice the weaker party or an obnoxious individual. Hence it is that such democracies have ever been spectacles of turbulence and contention; have ever been found incompatible with personal security or the rights of property; and have in general been as short in their lives as they have been violent in their deaths. Theoretic politicians, who have patronized this species of government, have erroneously supposed that by reducing mankind to a perfect equality in their political rights, they would, at the same time, be perfectly equalized and assimilated in their possessions, their opinions, and their passions."
>
> **James Madison**
> Federalist 10
>
> *Author's note: "10" is the "must-read" of all the Federalist Papers*

The founders feared what Alexis de Tocqueville later referred to as "the tyranny of the majority." A democracy is a government controlled by a majority of the voters, who, as history has shown, will eventually opt for riches instead of justice; the founders knew this. Their republic was designed to hold the force of law over all popular pressures by placing many activities of government above simple majority-rule.

Tying into our republican design is the only guarantee in the Constitution (the answer to the second question) which is found in Article IV of our Constitution, and states, in part:

*"**Section. 4.** The United States shall guarantee to every State in this Union a Republican Form of Government, and shall*

protect each of them against Invasion; and on Application of the Legislature, or of the Executive (when the Legislature cannot be convened), against domestic Violence."

Of course, having a republican form of government doesn't mean that only republicans should hold office any more than a democracy would demand that only democrats should hold office; the guarantee refers to a type of government.

The meaning of this guarantee is open to some debate. Why is the guarantee made to the states and not the people? Does the *"Republican Form of Government"* refer to every government in the United States? What constitutes such a form of government? (This issue is covered in greater detail in the final chapter, *Two Senates.)*

To answer the third question, the *Federalist Papers* were written by Alexander Hamilton, James Madison and John Jay. Hamilton and Madison helped write the Constitution; Jay was the first Chief Justice of the United States Supreme Court.

The *Federalist Papers* are a series of eighty-five essays that were printed in various newspapers, all written under the pen name *Publius,* in honor of Publius Valerius Publicola, a Roman consul who has been called a great statesman. *Publicola* meant "friend of the people."

At the time of the writing of the *Federalist Papers* (1787-1788), the people of the State of New York were debating the ratification of the new Constitution. From the beginning, the citizens of New York were lukewarm about the idea of the new national government. James Madison noted that those citizens were somewhat happy with the current government under the Articles of Confederation because it gave their state great powers and no national taxes. Why would they want to change that?

Adding to that problem was the fact that New York's delegation ended up with only one man, Alexander Hamilton. The other two, John Lansing and Robert Yates, had left the convention in protest of a totally new government. New York lacked an official delegation, so the writers of the Constitution needed to sell the people in the State on the idea of this new government.

Messieurs Jay, Hamilton and Madison used their writings to explain to the people why the Constitution was written the way it was, how it was to work, the security it gave the new nation and the protections it gave the states. Altogether, these articles became known as the *Federalist Papers* and the authors of each paper eventually became known.

The *Federalist Papers* are still used to argue the constitutionality of various federal processes. They provide a wonderful example of the writing style, principled thinking, substance and intelligence that fostered the Constitution. Although the writing is complex (a sentence can be as long as a paragraph) and the vocabulary strong, reading these papers is a unique adventure that will surely broaden anyone's horizons.

Criticisms of the New Constitution:

After the new Constitution was offered to the states, spirited arguments against its ratification were presented by a group of persons now known as the Anti-Federalists. Included in this group were persons such as Robert Yates and Patrick Henry. It is believed that Yates wrote under the pseudonym "Brutus." What follows is an excerpt from one of Brutus' writings where he fears the loss of state powers as the federal government's grows:

> *"Besides, it is a truth confirmed by the unerring experience of ages, that every man, and every body of men, invested with power, are ever disposed to increase it, and to acquire a superiority over every thing that stands in their way. This disposition, which is implanted in human nature, will operate in the federal legislature to lessen and ultimately to subvert the state authority, and having such advantages, will most certainly succeed, if the federal government succeeds at all. It must be very evident then, that what this constitution wants of being a complete consolidation of the several parts of the union into one complete government, possessed of perfect legislative, judicial, and executive powers, to all intents and purposes, it will necessarily acquire in its exercise and operation."*

Brutus
October 18, 1787

This criticism could apply to any government. Brutus' writing *"that every man, and every body of men, invested with power, are ever disposed to increase it"* brings forward more criticism of man in general more than it does of the proposed Constitution.

The anti-federalists never put together a rational alternative to the proposed Constitution; but, they were successful in getting the new government to have a bill of rights.

The upcoming *Bill of Rights* had its own opponents, including the eventual writer of the first ten amendments himself, James Madison. One of the better arguments presented against the *Bill of Rights* was penned by Alexander Hamilton in *Federalist 84*:

> *"I go further and affirm that bills of rights, in the sense and to the extent in which they are contended for, are not only unnecessary in the proposed Constitution, but would even be dangerous. They would contain various exceptions to powers not granted; and, on this very account,* ***would afford a colorable pretext to claim more than were granted."*** *(Author's emphasis)*

How many times have we heard people claim to have rights that are not found in the Constitution? Again, the Founders knowledge of human nature and its desire to manipulate law gave us warnings of things which would infect our politics of today.

Of note is how James Madison was given credit for the *Bill of Rights*, but how much the Amendments were similar to the *Virginia Declaration of Rights* that were written by James Mason in 1776.

Mason was one of the delegates to the Constitutional Convention of 1787, but ended up opposing ratification of the new document because it had no bill of rights. His opinion caused him to lose some valuable friendships, most notably with George Washington and James Madison. One wonders if that is why Mason was never given more credit for our Bill of Rights.

Short of a Perfect Union:

The *Republican Form of Government* originally designed by the founding fathers is the government described earlier in this chapter as "the government of liberty and law." Some forces are now changing it into a "providing government" despite the inherent dangers that such a system poses to a nation and its people.

Our original Constitution did leave room for an important improvement to liberty — the abolition of slavery, which was later accomplished by the Thirteenth Amendment.

During the Constitutional Convention of 1787, the slavery issue caused great problems among the delegates. It became obvious that some states would not join the new government should the Constitution outlaw slavery.

If the convention failed to unify the States, the nation would have been in danger of splitting into two, three or four alliances. An independent Southern nation would have continued slavery and been susceptible to foreign influences. Worse still, there were many lands in the West that awaited the sort of governance that the Articles of Confederation could not provide. This again, would invite foreign influences.

The delegates knew that the future of the union would be in great danger if our nation did not move to a stronger national government.

Sadly, slavery was a necessary element in the formation of the full nation, yet the new Constitution was a step in the right direction. It gave the government the ability to limit and finally outlaw slavery, a power that the Articles of Confederation lacked.

The Foundation:

A basic rule of logic advises that for a point to be valid, the premises that support that point must also be valid. Keeping this in mind, one of the most important questions I ask during a political argument concerns a person's main premise: "What is the foundation of your political philosophy?" Any politically active person should have a foundation, and, therefore, a ready answer to that question. My foundation is easily identified: our Constitution. There are people who have not thought about a foundation for their political opinions. I have often heard answers such as "Government should care for the people," or "Government should protect the environment" or "Government should protect our rights." Such statements miss the first and most important reason for the national government of any country: to protect the nation and its people from invasion.

There can be a problem associated with the defense of a nation. If the government has done its initial job of national defense well, to a point where the citizens take their security and safety for granted, people may then end up wanting their government to change its most important purpose (the foundation) to something different, such as the personal care of the citizens. This will change the entire design of the government.

Today's political climate shows that this abandonment of liberty and national defense is occurring. Despite the atrocities committed by governments and factions around the world, the increased presence of weapons delivery systems that are capable of leaping over continents and oceans in a few minutes, the increased threat of weapons that can kill an entire city in one shot, the fires of religious and political hatred that are fanned by some politicians of this very country, and despite the fact that these realities are brought into the citizens' homes by daily communications, our security from foreign enemies is now the least of some politicians' and citizens' concerns.

Some Americans actually help our enemies in order to improve their political positions. Why would the people allow this?

Party Spirit:

Again, our country's founders understood the problems that could befall our nation. George Washington directly points out the dangers of *party spirit* in what may well be the best of the short writings of our founding fathers, his *Farewell Address.*

Our first president disliked the party system, writing:

> *"It agitates the community with ill-founded jealousies and false alarms, kindles the animosity of one part against another..."*

That was just the start of his criticism. He knew that people wanted their party to win, even if that victory was at the expense of the nation's security or liberty. We see that in his address — pay close attention to each word he uses:

> *"Let me now take a more comprehensive view, and warn you in the most solemn manner against the baneful effects of the spirit of party generally.*
>
> *"This spirit, unfortunately, is inseparable from our nature, having its root in the strongest passions of the human mind. It exists under different shapes in all governments, more or less stifled, controlled, or repressed; but, in those of the popular form, it is seen in its greatest rankness, and is truly their worst enemy.*
>
> *"The alternate domination of one faction over another, sharpened by the spirit of revenge, natural to party dissension, which in different ages and countries has perpetrated the most horrid enormities, is itself a frightful despotism. The disorders and miseries which result gradually incline the minds of men to seek security and repose in the absolute power of an individual; and sooner or later the chief of some prevailing faction, more able or more fortunate than his competitors, turns this disposition to the purposes of his own elevation, on the ruins of public liberty."*

Excerpt from **George Washington's**
Farewell Address, 1796

This was a stern, emphatic warning; it was not a gentle note on politics. Our first president was among the knowledgeable founders who were fearful that the liberties of man, which were protected by our own Constitution, would allow the seeds of tyranny to germinate on the grounds of hate-filled politics. Party-line citizens could willingly trade some of their liberty for vengeful provisions or self-enrichment if the situation presented itself. All they needed was a politician who promised a remedy for their financial problems, perceived victimization, needs or desires.

> "Government is not reason; it is not eloquent; it is force. Like fire, it is a dangerous servant and a fearful master."
>
> **George Washington**

As Washington noted, the party spirit can be rooted in the strongest passions of the human mind. This presents a substantial problem.

Once a faction starts the process of ridiculing others and a person within that faction accepts the attacks as justified and truthful, his ability to judge in an objective manner may have been lost. He has allowed his political leaders to inject a prejudice in his decision-making processes. He can become obsessed in finding the faults of others while ignoring a fair study of his own faction's faults. Everything that individual hears, sees and reads is colored by his personal perceptions of the evils of the other party. He succumbs to a process of validating his party's perceived intelligence and virtue while "confirming" the stupidity and mean spirit of his opponents.

Overcoming this Hatfield-McCoy feuding mentality is difficult, if not impossible.

Legalized Theft:

Providing governments often rely on a form of hatred for their existence. Remember, for a government of this type to give to some, it must take from others.

Obviously, the beneficiaries of a providing government do not want their goodies coming from children's cookie sales or donations that were meant to go to some orphans' hospital. So, the political opportunists who engineer the taking of money or property know they must make citizens believe that theirs is a noble cause: The money and property is being taken from those who "deserve" to lose their assets.

The leaders must publish propaganda to convince the people that their superior party is either protecting society from the greedy, unprincipled political enemies, or punishing opponents for their violations of social law; in this way, the "noble" government leaders establish their own form of justice.

Frederic' Bastiat wrote about this problem over 150 years ago:

> *"Self-preservation and self-development are common aspirations among all people. And if everyone enjoyed the unrestricted use of his faculties and the free disposition of the fruits of his labor, social progress would be ceaseless, uninterrupted, and unfailing.*
>
> *But there is also another tendency that is common among people. When they can, they wish to live and prosper at the expense of others. This is no rash accusation. Nor does it come from a gloomy and uncharitable spirit. The annals of history bear witness to the truth of it: the incessant wars, mass migrations, religious persecutions, universal slavery, dishonesty in commerce, and monopolies. This fatal desire has its origin in the very nature of man — in that primitive, universal, and insuppressible instinct that impels him to satisfy his desires with the least possible pain".*

Frederic Bastiat,
THE LAW, 1850

There is a point when the citizens' greed or sense of fairness affects the course of government. The desire for provisions from the government — Bastiat called it "legal plunder" — often causes the beneficiaries to turn their heads away from the incredible losses suffered by the targeted families that brings the citizens their plunder.

The desire for plunder is without end. Some people criticize the foundation of our government because it was designed in a way that enabled the founding fathers to keep their property. But that half-truth misses the fact that every government on earth or every person put in office had one of two intents: the preservation of private property or the taking of it.

The Oldest Question in Politics:

One of the questions that Plato addressed over 2,000 years ago was that of defining *justice*. Among other things, Plato believed that a person keeping the fruits of his own labor exemplified justice, and there are citizens who still work for this style of justice. But there are some whose idea of justice involves taking things from others under the excuse of authority by using programs such as Affirmative Action, citizens with disabilities laws or claims of environmental and economic justice.

If a citizen receives handouts from his government that were seized from innocent people, would he care? Despite many citizens' claims that they would care, history has proven the opposite.

The profit motives within party politics is one reason it has failed to "modernize." There is just too much money in politics and too much power given to those leaders who promise to provide *legal plunder* to citizens in exchange for their votes. And, there are too many citizens who are willing to accept this plunder.

The complications are obvious, but now that we have learned some of the basics, let's try to make politics sensible.

4

The Constitutional Initial Point

"... [T]he habits of thinking in a free country should inspire caution in those entrusted with its administration, to confine themselves within their respective constitutional spheres, avoiding in the exercise of the powers of one department to encroach upon another. The spirit of encroachment tends to consolidate the powers of all the departments in one, and thus to create, whatever the form of government, a real despotism."

— **George Washington**
in his Farewell Address

What is proposed within this chapter is a system that, at first, may be as complicated as surveying itself. But there is a solid reason for its discipline: we do not want to get lost amid all the personal centers. Proper detail and structure is necessary if we are to advance our political debate past our current tangled mass of generalizations and the problems caused by their use.

The following system has a niche for every possible political proposal or law. It has a discipline that will allow a person to map out any political act, relative to our Constitution.

Three *Political Centers* are discussed in these chapters:

- ***The Constitutional Initial Point:*** the Constitution of the United States is the defined center. From there we work to the left and right.
- ***The Personal Initial Point:*** its author places one subject in the center and works within a graph of the their own design. Its design is open to any artistic rendering, including asymmetrical design. The Author may be an individual, political party or a faction.

- ***The Generalized Political Center:*** is used by most of our citizens and the media. It places the conservatives on the right, the liberals on the left and the moderates (the mainstream) in the middle. This center welcomes variable principles and inconsistent applications of law and its enforcement.

The *Generalized Political Center* and the *Personal Initial Point* will be studied in the next two chapters.

The Constitutional Initial Point Setup:

This system is based on law and is consistent in its placement of political theories and laws. As such, it has many differences from the personalized and artistic systems that many of us now use. For the reader to move from a personalized and comfortable artistic system to a regimented and disciplined system may not be an easy step; it's a big change.

The graph of this system is simple. It starts with a center that works as the initial point. From that center we have the left side and the right side.

1. The graph is composed of a horizontal line with a small block in its center that represents our initial point, the Constitution.

2. The lines from the center to the extreme right and extreme left are of equal length.

3. The center block represents the Constitution of the United States and its Amendments; our initial point.

4. Any **proposed law or constitutional amendment** is placed on the line outside the center block.

5. Some current laws will also be placed outside the center block (as explained in point number eight).

Working from the Center:

First, we set the Constitution in the center; this is the initial point. From that center we have a line representing the right and left sides of the political graph.

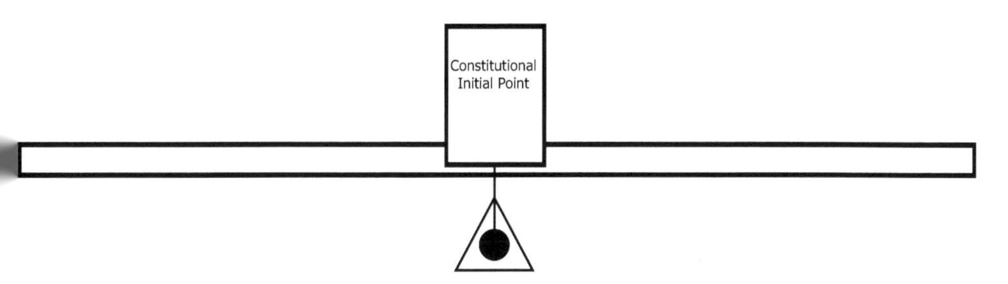

6. A foundation concerning the character of this line must be set. Since the Constitution is law, anything else that is put on the left-to-right line will also involve law — active laws or proposed laws.

Right or Left?

There are two basic ways to work with our Constitution.

- **Implicit:** Be respectful of the Constitution's philosophy and follow the laws, guarantees and proper procedures to change or enforce laws.

- **Artistic:** Show disregard or disrespect for the Constitution's philosophy and processes in order to change laws in artistic ways.

These two different processes explain the right and left domains of the graph.

(continued on the following page)

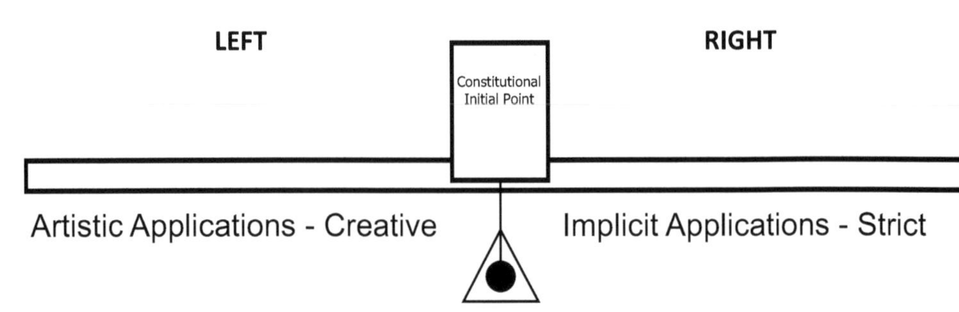

The Right Side:

7. The right side of the graph is the area for properly proposed changes of law that are in consonance with the Constitution's design as a **republic** of liberty and law, or for properly changing processes that are already included in the Constitution.

Proposed amendments to the Constitution that satisfy this requirement will be placed on the right side. Proper changes to punishments for violations of current constitutional law will also be placed on the right side.

For example, a proposed amendment to the Constitution to make English the official language of the United States government would be put on the right side of the graph; it involves only the federal government, is a properly proposed amendment to the Constitution, and is in consonance with the original design.

The Left Side:

8. The left side is the domain for proposed law or current government processes (based on laws that are exo-constitutional) that are outside of the Constitution's design for a *Republican Form of Government*. In short, anything that does not fit the strict standards for placement on the right side will find its position on the left.

Social Security, Medicare and the Federal Department of Education are not in the constitutional design, so laws and processes that relate to these bureaus will fall in the area left-of-center.

To fully illustrate this concept, I will use a controversial topic as an example. Any constitutional amendment to outlaw abortion would be on the **LEFT** side, because there is nothing in the Constitution about abortion. Therefore, **laws** concerning the procedure would fall under the Tenth Amendment's granting of powers **to each State**.

Notice that the left side will contain all proposals **and** current laws that are outside of the constitutional design of a *Republican Form of Governm*ent.

Activity:

9. The right area is legally inactive. It is made up of proposals, nothing else. Once one of those proposals becomes constitutional law it moves inside the center block, where it becomes active law.

10. The left side comprised of proposals or active law. Laws relating to any exo-constitutional facet, such as Social Security, may be legal, enforceable and actionable, but unless they become part of the Constitution (via amendment) they will stay on the left side.

Making the Initial Point a POINT:

At this stage we become more detailed. Keep in mind that the initial point — the constitutional center — is set in this manner:

- The exact law as stated in the Constitution
- The philosophy as defined by the *Federalist Papers*

Other writings, such as Washington's *Farewell Address*, have no consideration in this matter, even if they agree with the two above elements.

Distances – Intensities:

From the specific initial point of the constitutional center, we must strive to portray accurate relationships and distances.

When people say that something is extreme left or right-wing, they are usually referring to the intensity of their disagreement or dislike of an individual, act or law; this characterization is based on their personal center. The constitutional center works with law, not emotion, and gauges the intensity accordingly.

The least of the intensities is indifference, where the law or the individual does not care about something. The opposite of indifference – no intensity – is extreme intensity; it involves death for a crime. These two intensities set the ends of the political graph.

Our legal system already has a good framework for the other intensities. Each law brings with it a punishment that is correlated to the intensity of the infraction. The worst type of crime (murder) carries the worst punishment, usually death or life imprisonment.

The lesser infractions carry lesser punishments, if any at all. So, we have punishments ranging from no action – to – the taking someone's life.

Drawing It:

Each of the blocks outside of the center represents a spread of activity, starting from nearest the center and increasing in intensity as it moves outward. We work with the increasing intensities in a step-by-step process, starting from the center and working to the extreme ends.

The following samples depict the areas to the right of the initial point. Areas to the left of the initial point will be the same, but flipped 180^{0} to the left.

The first section in the graph represents the absence of concern (*Indifference*) — to — an entity (either a person or a government) being concerned but allowing the behavior; that is *Tolerance*.

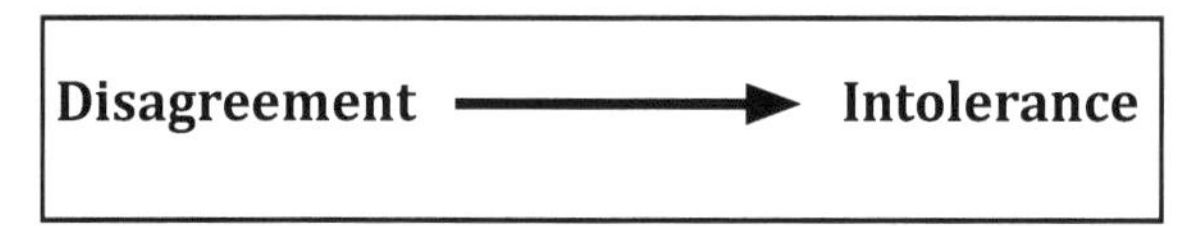

The second section starts at voiced disagreement, then moves to areas of some activity; this would range from avoidance to active protests. It is the last area of non-governmental involvement.

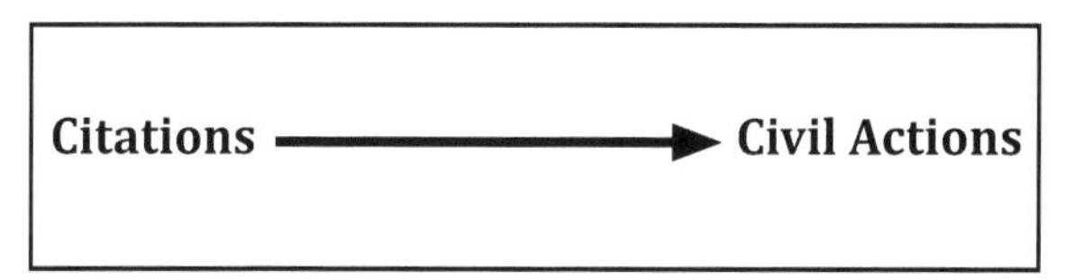

The third section is the first area of government involvement. Ranging from parking tickets to expensive civil court actions, loss of some property or reputation can be involved. In exceptional cases, a great deal of money or property may be at risk.

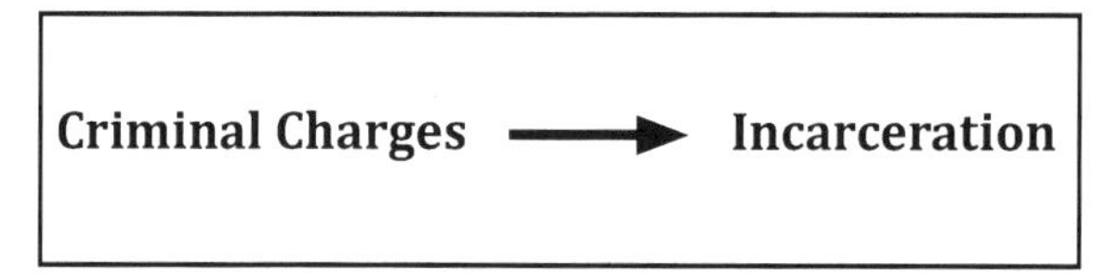

The criminal blocks (the next three sections) involve serious involvement by the authorities. From loss of property and other assets to imprisonment and the loss of rights, a citizen can lose everything they have, including their life.

We now put these together for the graph on the following page.

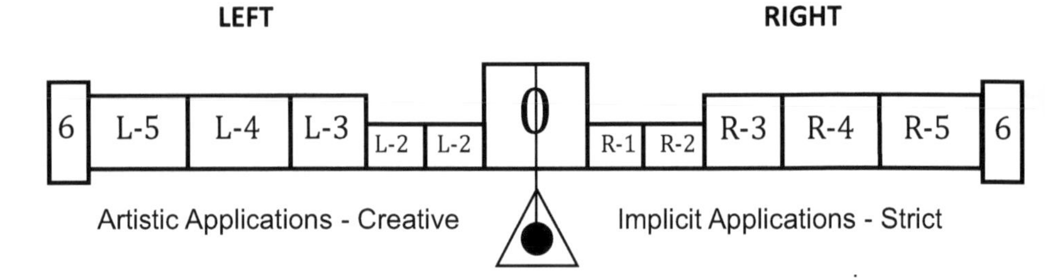

0. **The Constitutional Center:** the initial point

1. **Indifference to Tolerance:** ranging from neither the citizen nor the law caring about certain behavior — to — not liking the behavior, but allowing it.

2. **Public Disagreement to Intolerance**: ranging from avoidance, social out casting and shunning —to — active protests, ridicule and informal accusations against parties or persons.

3. **Citations to Civil Court Actions:** this is the first area of government involvement, represented by a higher box. It ranges from citations and small claims court actions — to — official hearings, expensive legal actions and civil trials that may cause the loss of money, property and employment.

4. **Criminal:** ranging from loss of rights and/or property — to — imprisonment of less than five years.

5. **Long Imprisonment:** from five years to life imprisonment

6. **Execution:** loss of life (extreme)

The points of this graph start out with the citizens or the law **not caring.** From there they travel to the most extreme of punishments, **execution**.

Positioning a Proposed Law:

A constitutional amendment to make English the official language of the U.S. government would be plotted inside section **R-3** because:

a) It is a properly proposed constitutional amendment that is in harmony with the original constitution's design and intent; therefore, it should be on the right side.

b) Section 3 is the first area of government involvement.

c) The change in law addresses procedure, of which the punishment for a violation is minimal.

If the proposed amendment were to make it a capital crime to violate the English requirement, the plot would be in Section R-6, the extreme end of the right side.

According to this constitutional center, an extremist is a person who advocates the death penalty for the violations of certain acts or laws. This differs greatly from the plotting within a personal center, which will be discussed in the next chapter.

Plotting on the Left:

If I filed an expensive lawsuit charging the City of Los Angeles with a violation of my rights because I believed the small crosses on their city seal violate the establishment of religion clause of the First Amendment, the action would be plotted left of center.

a) Because the First Amendment to the Constitution protects the *free exercise of religion*, the left is the proper side of the graph for this lawsuit.

b) The act is beyond intolerance, so it is beyond section L-2.

c) The fact that it is a civil suit would place this act within section L-3. If the suit were expensive, it would be on the extreme side of that section.

Clarity:

A constitutional center acting as the initial point delivers an objective way to consistently determine the plot points of proposed or active laws.

As we will now see, the same cannot be said for the personal initial point.

5

The Personal Initial Point

"...[A]n association of men who will not quarrel with one another is a thing which never yet existed, from the greatest confederacy of nations down to a town meeting or a vestry..."

Thomas Jefferson
- *in a letter to John Taylor*
June 4, 1798

Each nation will have its own constitutional center based on its own laws. But within that nation, there will be people who selectively apply the laws — or their belief in which laws exist — to develop their own political graph. This practice will result in a series of personal initial points, the foundations of which will vary with the emotions, knowledge and prejudices of the various designers.

As we will see, the difference between these personal centers and the Constitutional Center can be substantial.

Consider what would happen if each landowner in our nation used their personal initial point to determine property lines. No matter how well your lands were measured and no matter what was on the deed of the property you purchased, it all could be wiped away by one change in the initial point. It would be madness.

Yet, that is precisely what we are doing with our laws.

Personally Speaking:

Here is the makeup of some philosophies within a sample personal center:

- Every search must have a warrant.
- Majority rules in every issue.
- Unemployment payment is a right.
- Guns are only for the police and military.
- Education is a right.
- There should be a popular vote for president (abolish the electoral college).
- Absolute separation of church and state is a must.

Not one of these items has a constitutional foundation, so all would be outside of the central block of the constitutional center. Each element could be graphed separately, so we can pick any one of the items and work with it.

Drawing It:

The following graph is entirely artistic. It may be symmetrical or asymmetrical; it may have different gradations for the elements from one side to the other; it may include a section or two on one side and omit them from the other.

For this example I will use *the absolute separation of church and state*, a common stance among people who dislike the political activism of religious organizations.

Since this personal center concerns religion and government, the sides of the graph must reflect that fact.

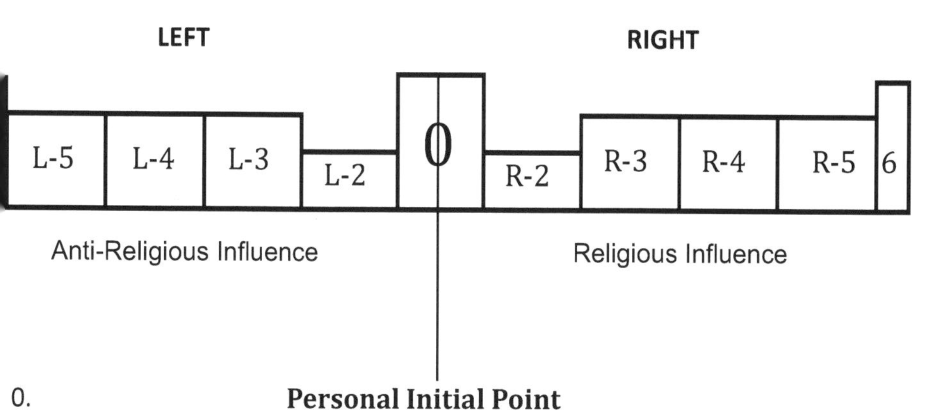

0. **Personal Initial Point**

1. **Indifference:** Does not exist in this personal graph; this person is very concerned with religious activism

2. Disagreement — to — Intolerance: In this case there may be more intolerance than disagreement.

3. Citations — to — Civil Court Actions: Intolerance quickly moves to action, often resulting in lawsuits or agreeing with those that are filed.

4. Criminal: The religious (right) theocracy or atheist (left) bureaucracy becomes part of government, punishing those who fail to comply with the new edicts.

5. Long Imprisonment: The punishment increases for religious or non-religious opinions and practices.

6. Death: Killing citizens because they are not of the official religion (right side), or because ***of*** their personal religion (left side).

Now we have a graph that reflects the beliefs of its designer. Their strong disapproval of religious invasions into activities of government is shown by the absence of the first section bordering their center; this person carries no indifference and very little tolerance when active religions are concerned.

Uneven Graph:

The previous example is symmetrical, but the sides on a personal graph do not have to be. Here's an example of an asymmetrical personal graph:

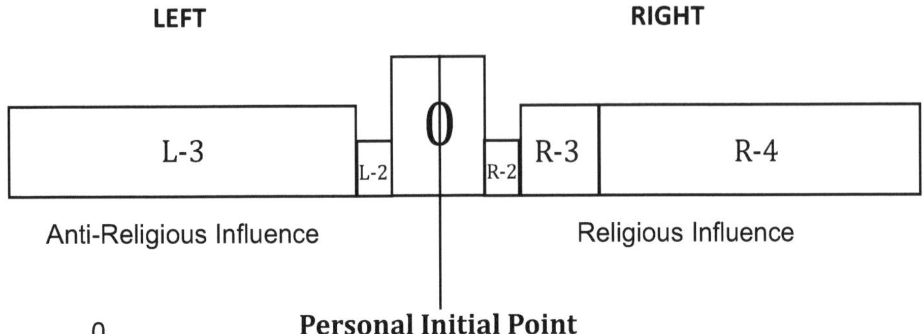

0. **Personal Initial Point**

1. **Indifference:** Does not exist in this personal graph; this person is very concerned with religious activism and believes the pro-religion forces are active as well

2. Disagreement — to — Intolerance: Very small

3. Citations — to — Civil Court Actions: The intolerance is quick to find legal remedies and force to silence the opponents

4. Criminal: The religious theocracy becomes part of government, punishing those who fail to comply with the new edicts.

Here the designer continues their concern of religious activism by leaving no blocks for indifference to tolerance. But the knowledge of their own opinions contrasts sharply with their beliefs of what they fear the religious activists think.

The designer poses themself as an activist, but not one who uses criminal laws to enforce their opinion. But they strongly believe that the religious people will use the substantial force of criminal law to enforce their religious opinions.

Are these fears valid? No; not without a constitutional amendment.

Competing With Churches:

Often, a *personal center* will hold miscellaneous systems of a government caring for its citizens, such as health care, disaster relief and welfare payments. Aside from the citizen reaping the benefits themselves, this increased government involvement will free the person from what others would normally consider to be personal obligations, such as donations to the poor, care for the needy, voluntary work to benevolent organizations, etc..

When the government cares for "victims," it turns the citizens into pseudo-philanthropists by using their tax money to deliver that service. The citizen then does not have to expend their own personal funds on causes of humanity; perhaps they do not want to. They would rather spend their money on themselves instead of donating to charities.

The side effect of this "benefit" is that those who are opposed to such government philanthropy — those who believe in personal involvement and expenditures — can be easily portrayed as mean-spirited and insensitive. The fact of the matter is that the people who believe in government philanthropy are not helping anybody but themselves. They are forcing **others** to donate to causes by using the force of law. That is not much different than an official government church.

The question of good government versus bad government was answered during the creation of this person's personal center. The designer makes up this system to compliment themselves on their knowledge and good character; it embodies their definition of justice and fair play; it also shows their fears and prejudices.

Comparing the Positioning:

Positioning this personal center within the graph of the standard *constitutional center* brings out an interesting model.

(continued on the next page)

Since the designer of this particular personal graph believes in the strict separation of church and state, leading to costly lawsuits against religious organizations, their position within the constitutional center model would be on the far left side of L-3, indicated by the **spike** drawn through that area:

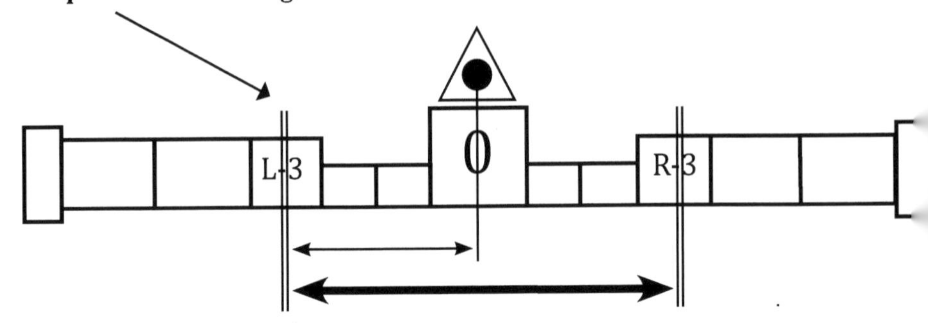

Notice the difference between this Personal Center's position and that of the constitutional center — indicated by the higher of the two horizontal arrows.

From the perspective of this personal center, a person who believed in the constitutional protection of the free exercise of religion - a centrist - would be far to the designer's right.

Even more striking is the difference between the spike through L-3 and the spike in position R-3, indicated by the lower (heavier) arrow. R-3 is the position for the act of using lawsuits to support the constitution's protection of the *"free exercise"* of religion.

As we can see, the subjective positioning of this personal center is the reason those who are intolerant of religious activists say that those activists are *"right wingers."* From their personal perspective, their religious-political adversaries are **far** to their right. But from the constitutional initial point, they are in the center.

Emotional Model:

There is another way to work with a personal center: emotion. This may be used when the designer does not address the issues by legalities or punishments, but my their intensity of like or dislike.

Their graph would be a simple line with a positive and negative side. The distances would be determined by the intensity of their emotion. If the designer heavily disliked a group's views, they could properly claim that they are extremists -- from a personal perspective.

Mutations:

When the authorities who are charged with the interpretation and application of law and its enforcement willingly work from a personal center instead of the constitutional center, they can use their personal philosophy and powerful positions to destroy the original design of a government.

Once a person swears an oath to preserve, protect and defend the Constitution of the United States, he or she should be held to that oath and exercise prudence when appointing proxies who can use their official seats to support or mutate the Constitution.

6

The General Political Center

"The Senators and Representatives before mentioned, and the Members of the several State Legislatures, and all executive and judicial Officers, both of the United States and of the several States, shall be bound by Oath or Affirmation, to support this Constitution..."

—Article 6,
Constitution of the United States

The *General Political Center* (GPC) is the political graph that most of today's media and major political players use when they categorize persons or acts; conservative is on the right, liberal on the left, moderates (or progressives) in the center.

It is a *center,* not an initial point. This is because law (which guides the Constitutional Initial Point), or a single person's philosophy (the foundation for the Personal Initial Point) may be specific. But beliefs within a culture are broad, competitive and subject many philosophies. This center accommodates all of these variables, making it broad and subject to constant change.

Design and Function:

There is a pragmatic reason for this center's presence. A proper constitutional foundation restricts the size of government. So, those who seek riches and benefits from the government need a tool of persuasion that will provide an alternative to a constitutional foundation; that tool is *The General Political Center.*

A faction's managers deliberately use this *center* to shift the dialogue and studies away from a government of constitutional design to one that is "mainstream."

The General Political Center avoids the Constitution and established law at its convenience. Instead of law, it uses the *mainstream* group-think to define the center by using gossip, assumptions, "rights," fear of victimization and such for its new systems of justice. Remember, laws can be "living and breathing."

The groups contributing to the steering of this center are the various forms of media, some political opportunists and those in education who do not properly educate the citizens on the constitutional foundations of our government. The concerted efforts of these groups end up posing a substantial obstacle to the proper workings of our republic.

Seduction:

To be secuced by this center, a person either has to lack the knowledge necessary for understanding a constitutional center, or know the elements of our Constitution and not wish to honor its laws or design. It is likely that there are more of the former than the latter.

But, it is easy to seduce people to this center when the movement claims that it and its members are altruistic, intelligent, and helpful – especially while it claims that its political competitors are the opposite. Continually reinforced, this is a powerful tool of seduction.

Aside from the above tools of ego gratification, payoffs play another important role. By using selective applications of law and its redefined standards of justice, the general political faction can offer benefits to the new followers. As history has proven, this is hard to resist.

When the General Political faction engages in these power-plays, it ignores the design and rewards of private accomplishment by presenting the expanded government as the champion of the new forms of justice and income. As the resulting government grows, it wraps its legal tentacles around more facets of our private lives and independent businesses.

Keep in mind that the followers of such factions truly believe that they are better, smarter and more principled than their political enemies. This is why the ridicule of others is so prevalent in their thoughts and communications.

Drifting Center:

As time has passed this center has allowed our government to keep moving away from the constitutional design; it is drifting to the left.

Think not? During his thirteen-minute inaugural address in 1961, John F. Kennedy said "Ask not what your country can do for you - ask what you can do for your country." This philosophy is the opposite of what his party members are now preaching, both in principle and in the short length of his speech.

The "mainstream" is subject to constant change. So, even if the party's name remains the same, its character of governance (democratic, republic, socialist, dictatorship) may change as well. This fact provides strong reason to **not** attribute a certain party's position as *left* or *right* – unless you are using the Constitution as a foundation.

Change and Caution:

As this center has mutated some of the processes of our government, one important definition has changed as well. that of *corruption.* Instead of being identified as a violation of constitutional design, *corruption* is now identified by the designers of the General Political

> "It may receive and promulgate accusations of all kinds against all persons and characters among the citizens of the state, and even against all inferior courts; and may judge, sentence, and condemn to infamy, not only private individuals but public bodies, etc., with or without inquiry or hearing, at the court's discretion...
>
> "It is not governed by any of the rules of common courts of law. The accused is allowed no grand jury to judge of the truth of the accusation before it is publicly made, nor is the name of the accuser made known to him, nor has he an opportunity of confronting the witness against him; for they are kept in the dark as in the Spanish court of Inquisition..."
>
> "Yet if an officer of this court receives the slightest check for misconduct in this, his office, he claims immediately the rights of a free citizen by the Constitution and demands to know his accuser, to confront the witnesses, and to have a fair trial by a jury of his peers."
>
> **Benjamin Franklin**
> *On the powers of the press*
> Memoirs of the Life and Writings of Benjamin Franklin
> 1819

Center as an undesired connection between their opponent's political movement and any supporting influence.

As an example, corporate contributions to those candidates who wish for government to abide by the Constitutional design may be severely limited or prohibited by strange applications of law. But free and favorable reporting of the GPC candidates by the national media are not be treated as a corrupt practice or as an in-kind campaign contribution.

Those who find comfort and benefits in these non-constitutional acts of government and the selective applications of law should be wary of the precedent such a center sets. They have empowered government to venture outside of its foundations, especially from its limitations of power and the rights that were once guaranteed to its citizens. When law means nothing, a foundation for tyranny is set.

7

The Primary Words of Politics "Liberal" and "Conservative"

"The accumulation of all powers, legislative, executive, and judiciary, in the same hands, whether of one, a few, or many, and whether hereditary, selfappointed, or elective, may justly be pronounced the very definition of tyranny."

— James Madison
FEDERALIST 47

Why do we have such great philosophical differences between the political parties when the politicians and the legalists are reading from the same Constitution?

If all of them have actually read the Constitution, the differences must stem from how they define the words and phrases in our founding document. It is probable that the differences between the parties are not due to the misunderstandings of the political leaders; they have a reason for their strict or artistic definitions.

Some politicians wish to maintain the Constitution's original intent and appropriately limit the size of government. These people are commonly referred to as *conservatives*. Some wish to change that foundation, either to a small or large extent, with the hope of garnering certain powers or benefits that are not within the Constitution's original intent and empowerment. These people are generally referred to as *liberals*. Some liberals may be mild, some will be extreme.

The above summation is a good start, but it is not specific enough. For clarity's sake, it is necessary to develop the definitions of these words to a greater degree — after giving them a firm foundation.

The Importance of Consistent Definitions:

Definitions influence our debates, which then influence the enactment and enforcement of our laws, which in turn influence the course of our government, i.e. economics, jobs and war. The problem today is that the artistic nature of our politics has left us with several definitions for important words, such as bipartisan, objective, discrimination, control, fairness, intolerant, prevention, rights, liberal and conservative. These words do not have a consistent application or solid definition that crosses party lines.

As a general guide, here are a few of the types of definitions that can be found in political dialogue:

1) Lexical: From a dictionary (lexicon)

2) Stipulated: Agreement between persons or parties

3) Persuasive: Equating a word with a judgment - such as "Abortion is murder"

No matter what definition is used, proper communication needs the stipulation, the agreement, between the involved parties as to the definition of the words they are using. Agreeing on the definitions of important words is the first step in logical communications.

Avoiding Failures to Communicate:

When an idea is **properly** communicated, all people involved will have the same picture in their minds.

If the initial message is a set of numbers (such as 1, 2, 35, 65) the message is easily defined, replicated and therefore understood by all parties. But if the message is a set of colors (such as white and blue), we will have a problem.

The white and blue issue will split people into two camps, those who make assumptions about the colors and those who demand specificity. For the latter group, a great field of ambiguity has opened before them. How white is the white? What is its Kelvin temperature? Which shade of blue is the *blue?* Is it sky blue, midnight blue, baby blue, periwinkle or some other artistic creation? For even greater specificity, the shade of blue may be identified by its wavelength, as if that would mean anything to most of the people on Earth.

Politics has the same analytical split. Some people are content with inaccuracies and sweeping generalizations. But, others need more knowledge. They need specificity — the accurate and proper detail conveyed in an understandable manner. It is a foundation for clarity, which makes true communication possible.

Liberal and Conservative Undefined:

Liberal has many definitions. In Aristotle's day the word denoted a giving and gracious manner. But, in his book *POLITICS*, Aristotle claimed that being liberal was an act of giving to others things that were your own. That's quite different from today's liberals.

When Niccolo Machiavelli wrote of a leader (a "Prince," in his words) being liberal, he used the term to refer to the politician's habit of spending lots of money - the opposite of being miserly. Machiavelli wrote that it was advantageous for a politician to portray himself as a liberal when he was running for office, but once in office being liberal was dangerous. Making promises was one thing, paying for them is another matter.

After studying writings of the founding fathers, I was left with the impression that they used the word *liberal* to denote a belief in liberty, such as liberty from oppressive government. Consider the time in which they lived. They wanted *change*; the liberty they received from their revolution against a powerful government was the *change* they sought.

But the *liberals* of today are different. They advocate more government involvement, more government control and more government power over every state in the union. This is not liberation from government, but the exact opposite.

Some people now define *liberal* and *conservative* in ways meant to compliment themselves and criticize their political opponents.

For example, one of the definitions I have frequently heard from self-identified liberals is that they believe they are people who are intelligent and receptive to new ideas and change. This claim is reminiscent of other ascensions of self-perceived superiors over inferiors in history. But we see that today's liberals advocate change until it puts their leaders or ideals in power. From that point on, further change is opposed.

Conservatives are often characterized as persons who are opposed to change and intolerant of new ideas, but most politicians who are identified as conservatives advocate changes in education, Social Security and government spending that today's liberals oppose.

Liberal and conservative are terms that can be used to identify party membership. But there are people who are fiscal conservatives while being social liberals; which party would that put them in?

Applying liberal and conservative to various acts produces other definitions. Would you want your company to account for its funds in a liberal or conservative manner? Even the most liberal politicians will manage their personal finances in a conservative manner, keeping their accounts in balance and calling a cent a cent and a dollar a dollar. That may differ greatly from how they manage this nation's finances.

If you put icing on a cake in a liberal manner, you would be applying more than is necessary or traditional. A liberal may be trying to apply more governmental control than is necessary.

Liberal, in many instances, means taking liberties from established or prudent procedures.

Others may define liberal practices as using connotations instead of denotations, or using slang and loose definitions instead of specific wording and consistent definitions.

Two Points:

The problems with defining *liberal* and *conservative* bring up two points. First, we understand these terms in a personal manner, employing our own idiom in order to define them to our own satisfaction. This results in definitions that can be as numerous as our citizens. Secondly, at present, there is no clarified meaning for these words standing alone; they work better when partnered with another word that pertains to some facet of government power, such as *fiscal conservative.*

The High Price of Inaccuracy:

Our government manages our national defense, our multi-trillion dollar budget, our Social Security programs, our laws, etc. Yet the politicians continue to work within a fog of multiple definitions and serial inaccuracies. The accumulated errors of this practice have yielded predictable results: Every sector of our government poorly manages its spending and is heavily in debt.

This ill-defined system has been a great advantage to any political faction that wants to hide its true costs or political consequences. Its temporary gain is this nation's long-term loss. There will come a time when our nation must pay its bills.

It's Serious, Jim:

Much of the citizenry have become comfortable with multiple meanings and vague phrases, which causes the politicians and the media to continue the practice. Again, we are ignoring the lessons of history.

In 1946, George Orwell (a.k.a. Eric Arthur Blair) addressed the subject of politics and inaccurate communication processes.

> *"Now, it is clear that the decline of a language must ultimately have political and economic causes: it is not due simply to the bad influence of this or that individual writer. But an effect can become a cause, reinforcing the original cause and producing the same effect in an intensified form, and so on indefinitely. A man may take*

to drink because he feels himself to be a failure, and then fail all the more completely because he drinks. It is rather the same thing that is happening to the English language. It becomes ugly and inaccurate because our thoughts are foolish, but the slovenliness of our language makes it easier for us to have foolish thoughts. The point is that the process is reversible."

George Orwell,
Politics and the English Language, 1946

To reverse this process we need to use clear and consistent definitions for our political words. Despite our inability to establish an official language, we can formalize the meanings of a few words, can't we?

Developing an Initial Point:

We already have a solid, common foundation from which we can build our political communication process. We will start with English, if there is no objection. From the foundation of English, we build to the foundation of our government and its politics: the Constitution. When we use our English language Constitution as the foundation for our political terminology, the terms *liberal* and *conservative* will have valid applications.

Step by Step Toward Objective and Subjective Law:

Again, we have to set a foundation.

People like taking liberties with some rules. For example, if any of us were cited for driving one mph over the posted speed limit we would be unhappy. In such a case virtually everyone would expect a bit of *liberty* — or wiggle room — from the letter of the law.

The intensities can vary, however; some people like a little wiggle room; others want a lot.

That wiggle room is the **un-strict observance of law** by citizens as they violate the law, and it can also be the **un-strict enforcement of law** by the authority as the law enforcement officer ignores the violation.

When the intent of law (or its enforcement) has been subjected to this wiggle room — a personalized view — it is properly defined as the **subjective** observance of law and the **subjective** enforcement of law. Those involved have taken liberties concerning the law's definition and enforcement.

So, it is defined as this:

> **Subjective Application —** When personal bias affects the definition, observance or the enforcement of the original law.

Subjective applications can mutate the original design of a government and its laws in several ways. Those using selective application can over-enforce the law by improperly using government agencies, hearing processes or various reporting procedures to punish or damage a political rival.

They can under-enforce the law by ignoring or minimizing the fair application of law and related procedures when protecting a member of their own faction.

Subjective application and enforcement of the law is a powerful political tool.

Objective Applications:

The consistent definition of the law within its intent and the consistent application of that law is its **objective** application. This consistency is similar to an axiom of mathematics: **A = A**. The words mean what they were originally designed to mean.

Under the objective application of law one party cannot change the definitions of law or modify the application of authority in order to punish political rivals or excuse the improper behavior of those persons they favor. Those who define and those who enforce the law will show no favors; laws will be equally applied to all citizens and all government officials.

> **Objective Application:** When law is strictly and consistently defined, applied and enforced.

The objective application of law is **usually** found when the acts or crimes are of a serious nature. Objective application is also found in the sciences, such as in the aforementioned periodic table of the elements. Some other professions (for example, surveying, navigation, accounting and timekeeping) use objective applications that provide us with reliable processes and data.

Mixing Applications:

When the law addresses procedural issues or low-level violations, we frequently find subjective applications or mixed processes of law enforcement. For instance, if our local police have a policy of citing all drivers who exceed the speed limit by six mph or more, we have a mix of the subjective application — the six mph wiggle room — and the objective application of law — citing all those who exceed the wiggle room.

At every level of enforcement we can find a power that allows subjective relief to favored people, from the personal prerogative of a law enforcement officer through various judges and up to the president, with his ability to grant pardons (except in cases of impeachment).

Serious Consequences:

An objective person either follows the law or properly changes it; a subjective person seeks to use wiggle room to change the definition and enforcement of law, usually to deal with an enemy or with a favored person.

It is the objective application of law and its processes that will provide and maintain justice and continuity in a society. Abuse of any of the enforcement powers can cause problems with a society's respect for the law.

Defining Liberal and Conservative:

Now that we've straightened out the subjective and objective applications of law, we can apply the terms *liberal* and *conservative* in relation to our government's initial point: the Constitution.

Liberal: a person who defines the Constitution's laws and applications in a *subjective* manner

Conservative: a person who defines the Constitution's laws and applications in an *objective* manner.

Whenever the words *conservative* or *liberal* are used in political discussions, especially in the United States, it stands to good reason to use them in a constitutional context, unless you want to hide something.

Going back to the constitutional center model, you will clearly see that the conservative applications are consistently on the right and the liberal applications on the left.

A Point on Clarity:

By providing a specific foundation for the terms *liberal* and *conservative,* this system will force many current associations and assumptions to be scrutinized from a constitutional initial point.

8

Elements Within the Initial Points

"It is necessary to guard ourselves from thinking that the practice of the scientific method enlarges the powers of the human mind. Nothing is more flatly contradicted by experience than the belief that a man distinguished in one or even more departments of science, is more likely to think sensibly about ordinary affairs than anyone else."[1]

Wilfred Trotter
Noted Social Psychologist

When a person abuses the meanings of words and phrases - especially in politics - you can rest assured that it is for money or power.

The initial points detailed in two of the previous chapters are made up of a combination of elements — words and phrases —that had a specific meaning and intent at the time they were written. If the original meaning of the words and phrases is maintained, the initial point will maintain its position as well. But when those elements are changed through so-called "modernization" (I prefer to call it *mutation*), the initial point changes as well.

The study of critical thinking is timeless. It transcends politics, often moving into our business and personal lives. From sales presentations to personal inquiries and newscasts, our understanding of critical thinking may save each of us some money, time and heartache.

1 This quote is taken from F.A. Hayek's book "The Fatal Conceit - The Errors of Socialism"

Deviations and Distractions:

Large books have been written on the subject of critical thinking, but this chapter will restrict itself to a short overview of a few fallacies and distractions.

Among the many fallacies, there are four that continually appear in our political debate. These fallacies are so prevalent in our media's reporting and the party communications that they need to be identified and understood by any objective person. These are the *post hoc* fallacy, the *non-sequitur*, the *straw man* and the *ad Hominem.*

The ***post hoc*** fallacy addresses a fault in a *cause and effect* relationship. ***Post hoc*** is a shortened version of *post hoc, ergo propter hoc.* The translation from Latin is "*after this, therefore, because of this.*" Here is an example:

> *Immediately after I stamped my feet on the floor, we were hit by a strong earthquake. Therefore, stamping my feet caused the earthquake.*

There is no true connection between the two events.

The second fallacy, the ***non-sequitur***, is the big gun of political hyperbole. The Latin translates to "*it does not follow.*" It denotes a lack, or absence, of a true connection between the premises and the conclusion.

> During president X's time in office the economy was good, the stock market reached its highest levels in history, the jobless rate was very low and personal incomes soared. This was president X's doing; it all happened on his watch. He is a great president.

A conclusion is assumed, not established, not proven. What was the real cause of the good economy? Did President X do anything that was directly connected to the economic boom? Or, did the boom occur in spite of President X's actions?

The ***Straw Man*** is when a person avoids the initial question and substitutes another issue. Politicians use this frequently. Here is an example:

> *Reporter: Newspaper Y reports that you were making fund-raising calls from government offices, which is illegal.*
>
> *Politician: The fact of the matter is that we have many problems with political fundraising, and it does not concern the location of a telephone. Soft money poses the greatest danger in political donations because it is unlimited in nature. We need to either ban soft money or severely limit its improper influence in our political system.*

Notice how the question was finessed (ignored) by the politician; he substituted another subject, thereby redirecting the argument. The term *soft money* is persuasive as well. The politician was **responding** to a question rather than **answering** it. This tactic is frequently used by crooks and trial attorneys as well.

And last (of these four) we have the **Argumentum ad Hominem;** attacking the person (or party) instead of arguing the issue. This can be blatant or indirect. First, the blatant version:

> *Reporter: Person X said that 2 + 2 = 4.*
>
> *Politician: Person X is a member of a radical religious cult! I'll never believe anything he says. Only idiots listen to him.*

Here we have a double ad hominem. At the onset the source of the statement is attacked; and then those who listen to the source are also attacked. Did you notice that the validity of the argument was never addressed?

Now the indirect version:

> *"I'm not saying that Politician M had an affair with his intern; but it sure seemed like he did."*

They are attacking the person while denying the assault – this is classic double-speak. Beware of any person who employs this sort of word manipulation.

Other Fallacies and Distractions:

Here I will name a few and lightly cover each item in hopes that it helps readers recognize fallacies and distraction tactics – instead of using them.

- **Begging the Question**: "Have you stopped beating your employees?" Here, the questioners assume something to be true in order to ask a question; they are assuming that the man is beating his employees.

- **Half-truths:** Manipulating an argument by purposefully leaving out important information within a fact. My favorite example is from Solzhenitsyn's book *The Gulag Archipelago*, where he wrote of several victims of a crime who could not identify any of the alleged perpetrators from a line-up. The reason the perpetrators could not be identified by the victims was because all the victims were dead; they could not identify anybody.

- **Wrongful Application:** is a combination of the ad hominem and begging the question, usually resulting in accusations such as racist, stingy, phobic, greedy, etc..

- **Sophism:** The history of sophism goes all the way back to ancient Athens, where professional educators flaunted their intelligence by making arguments that sounded stronger than the truth (does this sound familiar?). Sophism is covered later in this chapter.

- **Cultural Relativism:** Following the crowd or using numbers of people for validation instead of addressing ethics or justice. *It is mainstream thinking! Everybody does it!*

- **Intolerance:** Claiming someone is intolerant is the *straw man* mixed with the *ad hominem*; the term is reflective. When people have differences of opinion, why is only one side intolerant?

- **Projection:** Criticizing someone for engaging in bad behavior – which turns out to be the same as yours. The *intolerance* claim above is a good example.

- **Hypocrisy**: In politics this is usually a one-way street. If you set high goals and do not meet them, *hypocrisy* is used to mean you have failed, therefore subject to ridicule. *Hypocrisy* is not used if you set the lowest of goals, or no goals at all, then exceed them to attain a poor level of performance.
- **Selectivity**: Reporting (or listening to) only facts that are favorable to your argument while ignoring data that refutes or questions it.
- **Appeal to False Authority:** Citing a false expert or a popular person to promote your cause. If someone is an expert in one field, it does not make him an expert in other fields.
- **Trivialization**: Close to the **denial** of an act, both accomplishments and crimes can be trivialized or dismissed by people who wish to lightly acknowledge then immediately excuse certain events.
- **Serial Ignorance:** Instead of digesting an opposing point's validity, a person can ignore, ridicule or admit and quickly dismiss the point, then immediately offer more protests and accusations. As they do this they cannot measure the argument building against their case.
- **Lunar Landing:** Asserting an incredibly ridiculous and terribly criminal accusation; one that is so far from the earthly bounds of reason that the other person is forced to answer the charges, usually in a defensive manner. This is *begging the question* taken to an extreme.
- **Platitudes:** when a politician promises wonderful or miraculous results without having a defined course of action. *If I am elected, the economy will improve, crippled children will walk, every business will be successful, schools will be wonderful, etc..*
- **Ridicule:** Using all the above tools to promote disrespect for one's political rivals. In today's politics, the portrayal

of one party's intelligence and another's stupidity is the most common tactic.

- **False Dilemma:** Presenting limited options when others are available. The argument could be presented as a choice between two courses of action while many others are available, or it could be a matter of timing (*it's now or never!*).

- **Phony Phobia:** Claiming a disagreement is not a simple disagreement, but is an irrational psychological fear of an individual or his group. "Homophobia" is the best example of this application.

- **Hateful:** Is the language really hate-filled, or is the difference of opinion causing the receiver to hate the speaker? There may be more instances of the latter.

- **I don't recall:** This may be a true statement by a person, or it may be an act of perjury that is impossible to prove.

To maintain consistency in governance, the words that make up its laws should have consistent meanings.

If fallacies and distractions invade the foundation of an initial point, it sets the stage for a sequence of accumulated errors. In other words, just a slight remake of one word can have serious consequences by the time that a court rules on relevant laws.

Manipulation of the Masses:

Despite our belief that we are modern, intelligent individuals, we continue to fall for some of the oldest tricks in the long history of manipulation of the masses.

We now move into two areas of twisted logic that are used to gain power within our government and its associated politics. The fact that these two items are very active – and very successful – serves notice that our modern man is not so modern after all.

Sophism:

In a general sense, sophism is a brilliantly worded, well-presented, **invalid** argument that manipulates information and ambiguities to support fallacious reasoning.

Every fallacy and distraction of logic may be used to engineer a path toward sophism. Because we humans tend to use references from previous experiences, *trust* and *recognition* play substantial roles in the success of a faulty argument.

How it Works:

Instead of engaging in an objective and disciplined search for truth, the sophist will look for points that will support his desired outcome. He will select bits of information and manipulate their order and levels of importance so they compose an argument that leads the trusting audience to accept his position.

A stellar example of sophism is found in an old scientific model that lasted for a thousand years: the belief that the earth was the center of the universe. One well-respected scientist, known as Ptolemy (Claudius Ptolemaeus), tortured data and reason in order to support the "scientific finding" that he desired. His system involved a combination of the epicycle, the deferent and the equant to explain the "complex" motions of planets and the Sun as they revolved around the Earth.

Despite the ridiculous nature of the movements of the planets and the Earth, such as planets suddenly looping within their orbits, the public trusted the findings of the experts who delivered them; they were scientists after all! Trust them!

For sophism to work, the message must be delivered by a perceived authority (Ptolemy was a respected scientist) it must make some sense (the complex formulas seem to work) and it must lead to a conclusion that is pleasing to the audience (we're the center of the universe!).

Remember, sophism uses every fallacy and distraction to craft an argument. In addition to those elements, watch out for the use of the following words: smart, intelligent, green, stupid, greedy, stingy, mainstream, old, new, fair and intolerant. These words are often used as persuasive mechanisms; look beyond them to the real elements in the argument.

When sophism invades the fields of science and education for gains of power and money it can become a powerful weapon against truth and justice.

ACLUISM:

Has our system of justice become a system of legalities?

A strong case for this possibility is found within a process that I personally refer to as *acluism:* the filing of lawsuits for political and financial purposes with little regard to the genuine intent of the Constitution.

For *acluism* to work, the authority must be made to believe that a person is a victim of some "wrongful act" that is constitutionally protected. To do that, the Constitution's spirit will have to be circumnavigated by the chronic use of subjective applications and definitions of law. As one mutation can support a greater mutation, a chain of assertions is necessary for *acluism* to work.

An ideal example of the conservative/objective application of constitutional law versus the liberal/subjective application may be found in a legal battle concerning government and religion; it involves the Mount Soledad Cross, near San Diego, California, which stands above a Veteran's War Memorial.

The American Civil Liberties Union is (at the time of this writing) representing some people who had filed a lawsuit objecting to the cross being at this war memorial. The suit claims that the *cross* violates the "Establishment Clause of the First Amendment to the United States Constitution" and that its presence on federal land is unconstitutional.

Is the argument valid? The only mention of religion in our Constitution is found in its *First Amendment*, which reads:

> *"Congress shall make no law respecting an establishment of religion, or prohibiting the free exercise thereof; or abridging the freedom of speech, or of the press; or the right of the people peaceably to assemble, and to petition the government for a redress of grievances."*

Note: There is no mention of *the separation of church and state* within our Constitution, nor within the lawsuit concerning the *cross*.

A conservative/objective person does not confuse the *cross* with a *"**law** respecting the establishment of religion."* He believes its presence is covered by the *"free exercise thereof"* section of the First Amendment. End of argument.

How does the lawsuit ignore the *"free exercise thereof"* clause of the Constitution and arrive at its assertion that the *cross* is a violation of the First Amendment?

This argument is a good example of one slight mutation building upon another. Although it is not stated within the lawsuit, the argument must involve a chain of assertions that starts with the *cross* itself, which the lawsuit does claim to be a *Roman Cross*.

The chain will then have to move from link to link:

- The *Roman Cross* is one of a specific religion
- The *cross* is on government land
- That its presence is a promotion of a specific religion on the site (because of its *Roman Cross*)
- This required official government approval
- That is a legal proceeding

- That is a function of law, which "may" be construed as a law respecting the establishment of an official religion (Christianity) by our government.
- "Therefore," the *cross* is a violation of the "*Establishment Clause of the First Amendment to the United States Constitution.*"

Please note that in this argument, the literal wording of *"free exercise thereof"* from the actual Constitution carries **less weight and consideration** than the extended connotations that would make up such an argument and lawsuit.

The conservative argument claims that the liberal argument does not pass the A=A test. The *cross* is not a law; therefore, it cannot be a *"law respecting the establishment of religion."* It is a cross and nothing more. A conservative person views the liberal opinion as the product of accumulated errors.

Subjective Interpretation and *Acluism*:

Why would such a suit be filed? Are certain people genuinely mad that a war memorial, one that is dedicated to veterans who died fighting for this nation, has a cross? Are they so mad that they would risk a lot of money, take a lot of time and seek out a costly law firm to go to court and engage in legal warfare against the "malevolent" forces behind a Christian war memorial?

This brings up another question: Are forces trying to make atheism an unofficial national religion by filing lawsuits against Christian memorials but not against non-religious sites?

One might see fit to become "very angry" about all of this if he was guaranteed to make a handsome profit from a legal action. Is that what is happening here?

Let's follow the money.

Prior to 1976, each side of constitutional issue lawsuits paid its own expenses; money played no great role in the legalities. It was in that year that Congress amended the *Civil Rights Act of 1964* to make lawsuits profitable.

In the United States Code,[2] we can find the treasure gained from filing lawsuits that stem from a person's claim that his or her constitutional rights are being violated. It allows the prevailing party (if it wins) to collect attorney fees and damages from the defending party.

The attorney fees are one matter; the "damages" can bring the legal jackpot.

If a lawsuit is filed against a small township they may be able to send only one lawyer to argue. The plaintiffs may send six or seven attorneys, padding the price tag of the case. How can an individual, small church or township that has the nerve to argue for their constitutional rights, afford to do battle with a bunch of money-laden trial attorneys?

Are we seeing justice or intimidation?

Avoiding Change:

Some members of Congress have tried to change the loser pays everything and everybody rule, but the proposals can't get through the legislative system. In the 110th Congress we saw the formation of the '*Veterans' Memorials, Boy Scouts, Public Seals, and Other Public Expressions of Religion Protection Act of 2007.*' If it became law it would not have allowed damages to be awarded in cases involving religious words or symbols on veterans' memorials, public buildings, currencies or official seals. It would also protect the Boy Scouts in a similar manner.

The proposal seeks no side of the argument. It does not stop lawsuits or justice from being delivered. It allows for hearings on the matters and for decisions to be delivered. But it does stop the transfer of money for "damages" caused by a cross and forces a case to stand on its own merits.

Why does Congress refuse to pass this proposal? Is one party stopping and another party promoting this proposal? If so, is one party receiving most of the political donations from people who profit from today's system of legalities?

2 Title 42 > Chapter 21 > Subchapter 1 > § 1983

In case you're wondering about the answers to these questions, any research into those matters will open your eyes to how some campaign donations are infecting the present course of our government.

9

Political Navigation

"That no free government, or the blessings of liberty, can be preserved to any people but by a firm adherence to justice, moderation, temperance, frugality, and virtue, and by frequent recurrence to fundamental principles."

— George Mason
Virginia Declaration of Rights

It has often been said that if our founding fathers could see today's government they would be furious. They would have the knowledge to understand the difference between their Constitution's original design and today's application. Also, they had known many good men and women who died and lost their estates so their generation could deliver to this nation a government of liberty.

Our citizens have squandered that gift.

We could not have known those who died in the revolution; but, we can have the same understanding of the differences if we so desired. If there's a will, there's a way.

We have the tools that enable us to compare our government's current position with its constitutional foundation. We need to get off our political easy chairs and use them.

A Global Initial Point:

Again, we must return to the importance of *initial points,* but this time on a larger scale – with the element of *time* included.

About five miles East of London, England is the Greenwich Royal Observatory. The site was selected in 1675 by King Charles II, for the study of setting the world's longitudes and finding a way for ships to accurately determine their positions as they traveled around the globe.

The *Prime Meridian* runs through the courtyard of the Greenwich Royal Observatory. It is the initial point for all global measurements along an East-West line.

The navigators of old times knew they could find their latitude (North-South) and local (solar) time by using a sextant to measure the Sun's position. But, determining the longitude (their East-West position) was complicated because the Earth revolved; a measurement of the Sun's position alone did not provide enough information to determine a ship's longitude.

This is where accurate clocks, known as *marine chronometers,* entered the science. The ship's pilot set the chronometer at the time for the Royal Observatory in Greenwich Village. When the pilot compared the difference between the *Greenwich Mean Time* to his ship's *local solar time,* he could determine his longitude. The more accurate the clock, the more accurate the finding.

From fathoms to global positioning, mariners have always been serious about measurements. All the elements determining the positions were set upon firm, rational philosophies and consistent terminology; they were not subject to concepts that were "living and breathing" and did not change to cater to popular whim. Even when the element of time is employed, it is not used as an excuse to change the foundation of the science or to accommodate error.

Government is different only because we allow it to be so.

Navigation by Whim:

When a ship of state ignores valid information and relies on popular pressures for its navigation, it will engage in a variable course of law and justice, often decided by captains that are frequently changed.

As the course of government changes, the lives of its citizens and investments – involving incredible sums of money – change as well. So, the competition to be in command of any new course is lively.

If a good course was determined, plotted and followed, the command could focus on the efficient management of the nation. But when competitors use popular pressures to force the principles to change, the ship of state has to bother with continuous interparty problems and course corrections in order to satisfy the whims of the aspiring navigators.

Care and prudence should be exercised when any commander lays in a new course. Random, adventurous courses can guide any state into unchartered waters; or, worse yet, toward reefs of mismanagement and tyranny that will sink the ships of the sturdiest design.

The founders had great knowledge of those reefs and designed a course of government that would leave those dangers in the distance. Our course is now changing to that of a providing government. There are serious troubles on the horizon, if we care to look.

Navigation:

When we compare our government's current position with the *Constitutional Initial Point,* we can calculate the distance between the limited government guaranteed by our founders (the prime meridian of our government) and the drifting government that now "manages" our nation. There is no doubt that it is off course; it is surprising how far off course it is.

Before we place today's government within the model of the Constitutional Initial Point we need to consider the following facts:

- Legalisms and Court Cases: We have lawsuits that focus on areas that are already protected by the original wording of the Constitution.

- Assumptions of Power: The Federal government is heavily involved in education, social programs – including welfare – retirement programs for citizens and incredible retirement and compensation programs for government workers and members of congress.

- Violation of some exo-constitutional laws are criminal.

- Power Beyond Design: The Interstate commerce clause has been used to "justify" federal involvement in acts that were not mentioned in the Constitution.

With the government's heavy handed involvement in so many areas that were not in the original design we must conclude that from a constitutional perspective, our government is at least middle left. Some acts pertaining to these new government programs can be criminal, therefore the graph extends into section **four** of the left side.

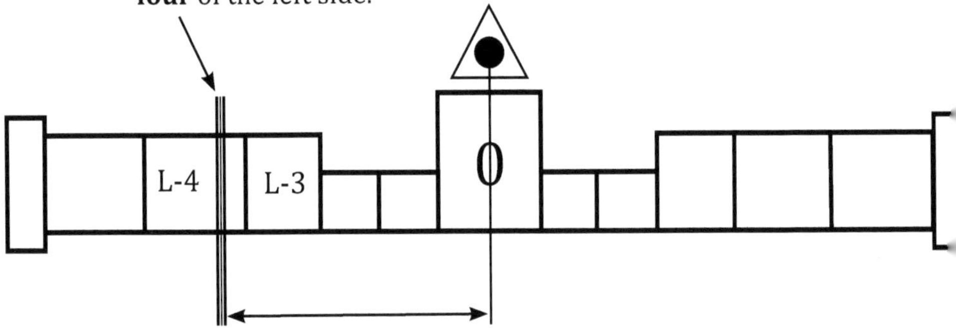

Our current government's position is so far from the *Constitutional Initial Point* that those who are in the center – the persons who believe in a constitutional government – are "right wingers" from the perspective of the members of our growing faction of anti-constitutionalists.

It is truly remarkable that a person with a constitutionalist viewpoint can now considered to be a radical — a person on the "fringe."

Point of No Return:

From our present position we can see two points of land. One is the land of a constitutional government. The other land is not an unknown; it is the land of socialism, pure-democracy, communism, dictatorships, monarchies, religious governments - all the terrible governments that our Constitution protects us from. It is the land that accommodates the tyrannies of those governments: legal plunder, nepotism, genocide, legalized intolerance, thought control and lost liberties.

Those officials who raised their hand and swore to "preserve, protect and defend" our Constitution have a duty to pilot us toward the land of constitutionalism. If they do not, we must hold them accountable.

The next chapter will study the cause of our errant course, and how it may be corrected.

10

Two Senates

"The first question that offers itself is, whether the general form and aspect of the government be strictly republican. It is evident that no other form would be reconcilable with the genius of the people of America; with the fundamental principles of the Revolution; or with that honorable determination which animates every votary of freedom, to rest all our political experiments on the capacity of mankind for self-government. If the plan of the convention, therefore, be found to depart from the republican character, its advocates must abandon it as no longer defensible."

— James Madison
FEDERALIST 39

When the founding fathers designed the Senate, they envisioned it as a chamber presided over by educated, prudent and principled gentlemen, not a room filled with politicians whose concern for our Constitution could be easily drowned by their party spirit. The Senate was designed to be a check on the abnormal growth of the national government that was managed by the states themselves. Its character and purpose were to be different than those of the House.

This chapter will discuss the mutation of our Constitution that turned the Senate into another House of Representatives, albeit with different rules. It will also examine how the accumulated changes caused by one terrible amendment to the Constitution have resulted in a government that is on the road to ruin.

The mutation is due to the Constitution's *Seventeenth Amendment*, which allowed for the direct, popular election of senators. That one amendment is responsible for setting the foundation for the incredible growth of our federal government, its distancing itself from the original constitutional principles, the loss of state influence in the legislative processes of the federal government and the increase of litigation in the United States.

Like a snowball that started rolling from the top of the mightiest mountain, the effects of the Seventeenth Amendment have grown larger over the years. Its size and force now dwarfs all of the original checks and balances in its path, crushing the wonderful design of our founding fathers.

The True Senate:

Let's start from the beginning. From the original *Constitution* we find this:

> ***"Section 3.*** *The Senate of the United States shall be composed of two Senators from each State,* ***chosen by the Legislature*** *thereof, for six Years; and each Senator shall have one Vote."* (Author's emphasis)

Consider the strengths of this design. If senators were placed in office by their state legislatures, their senators' behavior would be under constant supervision, chastisement and possible recall by their state officials. Those senators would not be driving off bridges, bouncing checks or recruiting people for racist organizations if they under such accountability, nor would they be running campaigns for reelection and opening up pathways for possible corruption by asking for campaign donations and various other favors.

The senators' focus would be on their states' powers and liberties instead of the deliberate growth of federal power at every state's expense. If a proposed law threatened state powers, state legislatures could tell their senators to cast their votes against the bill.

Adding to these points is a section from *Federalist 62*, by James Madison, wherein he stresses the importance of the nature of *senatorial trust*, which he says requires a "***greater extent of information and stability of character***."

Madison writes:

> *"It is equally unnecessary to dilate on the appointment of senators by the State legislatures. Among the various modes which might have been devised for constituting this branch of the government, that which has been proposed by the convention is probably the most congenial with the public opinion. It is recommended by the* ***double advantage of favoring a select appointment, and of giving to the State governments such an agency in the formation of the federal government as must secure the authority of the former, and may form a convenient link between the two systems.****"* (Author's emphasis)

Madison believed that the states should be linked to the federal government through their senators. He persuaded the States to ratify the Constitution by explaining that the **link** would enable them to manage the powers of federal government, not that they would be taken over by the same.

Moreover, in the same writing, we find this:

> *"Another advantage accruing from this ingredient in the constitution of the Senate is, the additional impediment it must prove against improper acts of legislation.* ***No law or resolution can now be passed without the concurrence, first, of a majority of the people, and then, of a majority of the States.****"* (Author's emphasis)

We can now see that the *impediment against improper acts of legislation* has been dissolved and that the initial design of the Senate with state-appointed members (Madison called it a "*well constructed Senate*"[3]), was changed by the *Seventeenth Amendment*.

---

3 In Federalist 63

"Amendment 17

> *The Senate of the United States shall be composed of two Senators from each State,* ***elected by the people*** *thereof, for six years; and each Senator shall have one vote. The electors in each State shall have the qualifications requisite for electors of the most numerous branch of the State legislatures..."*
> (author's emphasis)

Political power abhors a vacuum. Without the influence of the state legislatures, what would be left to control the Senate?

The New Senate:

In popular elections, any office-seeker knows that the best way to obtain or keep his high-paying, prestigious position is to provide government services and money to the voters; such a tactic, however, is antithetical to the original design of the Senate.

Vote-buying can only take place under an ever-expanding federal government that takes power from the states and an increasing share of assets from the private sector producers. This is why our federal government is now growing at a near-exponential rate. It is also why other serious problems have cropped up under the current government.

With any change in our governmental structure, Madison's remark about *stability of character* becomes vitally important. If a senator were to engage in his duties using anything other than our Constitution as the foundation for his policies, our nation would be put in a position where *stability of character* is the only influence preventing decay. Since the state cannot enforce that character, a party or faction may take its place — and this is exactly what has happened.

The voting records show proof of this decay; the Senate is now divided along party lines, not state interests. The driving force of this factionalism is financial gain and the distribution of assets to favored persons. The proper representation of state interests has been reduced to nothing; it is no longer a factor.

The new design also changed the Senate's role in their handling of constitutional amendments. A party-controlled Senate may block the states' possible approval or disapproval of any proposed amendment. In this regard, the Senate is the very opposite of the original design of our *republic*.

In addition, if political parties (rather than the states) exercise control of the Senate, decisions affecting miscellaneous appointments, including those of the judiciary, are also **infected** — and — I do not use that word lightly.

When a faction controls the Senate's process of confirming nominations by the executive branch, it can garner more power by promoting its own faction at the expense of the republic. It may confirm or reject the nominee through a vote by the Senate, which is fair; but it can kill a nomination by blocking the nominee's actual confirmation vote. A faction can do this by utilizing several loopholes that were developed as a result of its growing powers.

Within the last few years, such loopholes have been used to prevent important nominations and legislation from receiving a simple up or down vote.

Cloture:

In the old movie *Mister Smith Goes to Washington,* actor Jimmy Stewart stands on the floor of the Senate and speaks at length about principles that are very dear to him. The other senators have to let him talk because he is engaged in a process known as a *filibuster.* With it, a senator who has the floor may continue to "debate" the bill at hand to prevent a vote on a proposal or to hold the chamber from doing other business until the speaker gives way or gets his way.

But the long speeches were too much work; the new class of senators believed that there had to be an easier way. They eventually found a way that has become a powerful mate to the Seventeenth Amendment: *cloture*

Cloture became the new process used to identify whether or not the debate over a bill was finished in the chamber. With this rule, even if the discussions had ended and no more senators wished to speak, the debate would not "officially end" until **sixty senators** voted that it had ended.

With a simple rule change, the senators' jobs had become easier. They did not have to engage in long, tiring talk in an effort to block legislation. They could now block any bill or nominee by simply having a few senators not vote or not show up for work. The party-line politics had become far stronger.

Effects of Cloture:

Cloture has been used to block votes on judicial nominees and legislation, but there is one event in particular that I wish to cite.

Several years ago there was a bill that sought to keep Social Security funds in the Social Security program; it would have stopped congressmen from using those funds for various other activities and give-away programs. The bill was called the *Social Security and Medicare Safe Deposit Box Act.*

The majority of the House passed the bill, which then went to the Senate for a vote. The Senate's minority, in a party-line lockstep, blocked the vote on passage by using the *cloture* process.

The attempt to save Social Security funds failed.

Afterwards, the press reported that the measure could not get through the majority party-controlled Congress, despite the fact that it was the minority that had actually stopped it.[4] What's worse is that the man who ran for president in the following year blamed the majority in Congress for the bill's failure to pass; it was HIS minority party that had actually stopped it.

When coupled with the absence of state-appointed senators, cloture is a powerful political tool that benefits the party at the

4 This occurred during the 106th Congress. The bill was HR 1259. The Senate vote was 55—44—1; the votes were along party lines. The proposal needed sixty votes to pass cloture.

expense of the States, and, in some cases, the citizens as well. When a political party is given such power over another branch of government we may well have a situation that James Madison, in Federalist 62, identified as a despotic form of government.

Party On!

As one mutation eventually supports a greater mutation, the distance between the present government and the founders' original design of government continues to increase — along with our national debt. The resulting party control of the Senate subjects the federal government to the progressive erosion of constitutional law and principles, and to the internal invasion of other forms of government.

As a result of this Amendment, the senators of old, the "state's men," have become nationalized party politicians. The effects of their work now have the courts making decisions based on the accumulated loss of state power and the growth of a new political faction. The cancer is growing, the republican design has ended.

The Seventeenth Amendment brought about the greatest change to our government since the *War Between the States*. But this legislative war has been lost by **all** of the states, since they no longer have any official influence in the legislative processes of the U.S. government. Their influence has been replaced by party factions that receive their power from the voters' desire to take riches from the treasury and other citizens.

Killing the Tenth Amendment:

The state-appointed senators were arguably the guardians of the Tenth Amendment, which was designed to restrict federal growth. Without such senators, this amendment means little, if anything at all:

> ***Amendment X***
> *"The powers not delegated to the United States by the Constitution, nor prohibited by it to the States, are reserved to the States respectively, or to the people."*

This Amendment states our Constitutional right of limited government; the federal government can only do what the Constitution specifically empowers it to do.

In *Federalist 39*, James Madison states it eloquently:

> *"...its jurisdiction extends to certain enumerated objects only, and leaves to the several States a residuary and inviolable sovereignty over all other objects."*

We see the words **enumerated** and **inviolable**, but there is not one reference in the Constitution about running programs on education, science, retirement accounts, health care, etc.. Why is Congress expanding government beyond its stated and guaranteed design and why is the Judiciary allowing it?

Where Is the Republic?

The only guarantee in our Constitution, which concerns the United States being a *republic,* was briefly discussed Chapter 3; it is time to study that guarantee to a fuller extent.

To refresh the reader, the writers of the Constitution included this guarantee in *Article IV*:

> ***"Section. 4****. The United States shall guarantee to every State in this Union a Republican Form of Government, and shall protect each of them against Invasion; and on Application of the Legislature, or of the Executive (when the Legislature cannot be convened) against domestic Violence."*

This guarantee is still part of the Constitution. It has not been removed and is still in force. Instead of being trivialized into nothingness, this guarantee should be enforced.

Granted, there is a bit of ambiguity in the wording of this *guarantee*. Does it mean that:

a. The states alone are guaranteed to have a republican form of government?

b. All governments within the United States will be of the republican form?

c. The federal government makes a guarantee to the states that it will be a republican form of government?

These are all fair questions. But, it makes no sense to have mixed governments within the United States, especially if the federal government were to become a monarchy and hold the states to republican forms of government.

Moreover, if the Constitution had a popular Senate in its design, it may not have been ratified at all. The founders took great pains in designing a Senate that represented the State interests. This guarantee ensured a continuity of governments within the states who united under the Constitution.

Therefore, the latter two possibilities are the more reasonable and would fall within the original intent of the Constitution's authors and the promises made to those who ratified the new design of government. So we will continue with those two probabilities in mind after the following clarification.

Democracy:

People love the sound of the word *democracy*. It melds well with *power to the people* and *by the people, for the people* and other quips. It sounds wonderful. The people feel involved and empowered; but there has always been a good side and a bad side to that empowerment.

In a democracy, the majority of the voters decide the course of government. So, if fifty-one percent of the voters approve a law that requires the government to provide a free college education for any student, the government is legally bound to follow that mandate. Funding would be of no concern for the beneficiaries.

That sounds good, doesn't it? But history has proven that democracies are terrible governments, because the same formula can be used for good or terrible measures. For example, if Senator Stingy introduced a bill that proposed to kill the 1,000 richest people in the nation and distribute their assets to those who voted in favor of the legislation, the new law would be legal if it passed by a majority.

Moreover, once the people figure out how to vote themselves riches from the nation's treasury, they can become competitive about the power and try to take the assets before others do.

Since democracies embrace the rule of the majority, the will of the people can be stronger force within government than the oldest concepts of economic prudence or justice. It is as simple as that.

Republic:

History has provided many definitions of a *republic*, but the definition that matters to our nation is the one that the founding fathers gave us through the Constitution. Their design embodied the *republic* that they **guaranteed** to the states.

The founders knew that the departments of power must be separate and distinct if *liberty* was to survive,[5] so their republic provided three separate branches of government with checks and balances between them.

The legislature had a check that divided its influence; the House of Representatives represented the will of the people and the Senate represented the state governments.

The election of the president was managed by a process that avoided a national popular vote, hence the presence of the Electoral College.

Another check against majority rule is found in the amendment process, which required substantial actions by the legislative branch before the states could cast their votes; all the votes have to be far stronger than a simple majority.

History had warned the founders that when the majority realized their power, they often sought to take property or liberty from others. That is why the founder's design of a republic distanced itself from majority rule by placing a set of laws and procedures far above the will of the majority.

---

5 Federalist 47 by James Madison

A Great Contradiction:

As the effects of the *Seventeenth Amendment* grow along with the size of our government, we are objectively no longer a republic, but now a democracy with a few remnants of the republican design. The Electoral College is one of the elements; however, legislation has been repeatedly introduced in Congress to formally abolish it. As of this writing, there are three such proposals active in Congress.

The popular election of senators literally took the United States away from the founding fathers' design of a *"Republican Form of Government"* by removing the government's most important check on popular will, greed and mismanagement.

The *Seventeenth Amendment* has produced a government that now stands in direct opposition to the only guarantee in our Constitution.

Because the ratification of the Seventeenth Amendment did not remove the *guarantee* of Article IV, can a case be made that there is a contradiction **within** our Constitution? The original guarantee and the Seventeenth Amendment do stand in opposition to each other.

This sets a foundation for a state to sue the federal government, demanding that the Supreme Court abrogate the Seventeenth Amendment, thereby returning our nation to a government of senators appointed by state legislatures – in accordance to the original guarantee. This is not an outlandish idea; if there were other amendments that allowed invasion or domestic violence, surely lawsuits would be filed.

I believe that this is necessary. As explained in *Federalist 62*, the distinction between the two chambers was the vital ingredient in the founder's design of a *Republican Form of Government*:

> *"The improbability of sinister combinations will be in proportion to the dissimilarity in the genus of the two bodies, it must be politic to distinguish them from each other by every circumstance which will consist with a due harmony in all proper measures, and, with the genuine*

principles of republican government."

In other words, the closer the chambers are in their design (their sources of influence), the more *sinister combinations* we will have. Whatever those sinister forces are, they will seek power at the expense of our liberty.

The Remedy:

The hope of this book is for our political debates to involve accurate measurements, consistent definitions and proper constitutional government. Should that process come to fruition our nation has a chance to stop its suicidal slide and lift itself from our government's terrible mismanagement of finances and laws.

There may come a day when one or more brave states will file a suit against the federal government over the contradiction within our Constitution and the new government resulting from the Seventeenth Amendment. For the good of this nation, I pray that any such suit is successful and will return our nation to the Republican form of government guaranteed by our Constitution.

Acknowledgments

Many people contributed to this book without knowing, from those who argued politics in coffee houses to family members and friends, some of whose harsh rhetoric and emotional points repelled even the softest nudges of logic.

One does not like to fight with those who are dear to them, so I went to the books to find if my opinions were valid, or if I should pay greater attention to their argument.

It was a wonderful study.

Over some seven years of reading and writing, the understanding of our government found a way into my heart. Our original Constitution gave us a government that was as close to perfect as had ever been designed. As Sir Isaac Newton claimed that his studies were based on the works of the giants before him, our Founding Fathers studied governments before their own. They stood upon the shoulders of giants and became giants themselves.

I learned that our government's faults are not from the design, they are from poor administration. Think about it; the best car can be crashed and abused by a driver who desires to do so. Government is no different.

During my studies I had the support of many people, but I wish to thank some in particular. First is my family. My late Grandparents Zygmunt and Grandmother Frances, who had the fortitude to leave Poland for the promise of liberty in America; Grandpa George and Grandmother Antoenette, who chugged from Watertown, South Dakota to Phoenix in an old Model A Ford (Mom said that trip took forever).

It was in Phoenix that their daughter met and married my father, who was a lieutenant in the Army Air Corps and learning to fly fighter aircraft in 1944. That started our family.

Thanks also goes to my brothers and sisters, who supported or raged at my opinions and philosophy; and, my Father and Mother, who got me interested in politics and encouraged my studies and writings. And I wish to thank a special lady who continued to believe in my finishing this book.

There were key people who helped me remain objective by giving me a sounding board and good advice in presenting these arguments. My son, Michael Stadler, and his wife, Alethea, always gave me their time and open advice in preparing this book. A good friend, Bill Pierini, always had wise words and unfailing logic that tempered the emotions and the spirit of some of my harsher moments.

I also wish to thank the miscellaneous political pundits whose banter keeps politics entertaining. Of all these people there is one who has stood out. His gentle manner, love of knowledge, devotion to truth and fair play affected me; sadly it did not affect everybody. The few communications I had with him are now treasured, and I wish to thank him for what he taught not only me, but everyone who was willing to listen to him with an open mind: Tony Snow

Made in the USA
Charleston, SC
13 January 2010